CHILDREN OF THE LOST SEASONS

A Sequel to Daddy's Curse

Luke. G. Dahl

BASED ON TRUE EVENTS

This is a work of non-fiction. I have tried to recreate events, locales and

conversations from everyone involved. In order to maintain their anonymity in

some instances I have changed the names of individuals and places, I may have

changed some identifying characteristics and details such as physical properties,

occupations and places of residence.

DADDY'S CURSE 2: A Young Boy Who Has Survived Child Slavery Remembers...

This book is only to try to create awareness to these tragedies so they can be

stopped. No one involved in the creation of this book in any way approves

or supports this sort of harrowing deeds.

It contains strong language, explicit violence and scenes of a sexual nature

Editing by Stephanie Hoogstad

Designed by Rebecacovers

Beautiful minds inspire others

Written by Luke. G. Dahl.

First edition. August 19, 2018.

Contents

CHAPTER ONE

Losing Childhood

My curly hair and pointed nose were the only features Arban said I inherited from my Italian father. Even as a child, my grandfather would always taunt me by saying that my nose was erected as if to dominate the vibrant air, but every other feature I had was pure Mongolian.

My father, who I only knew as Ricardo, arrived in Mongolia as the secretary to an Italian diplomat. According to my grandfather, when he met my mother, the local girls made her the object of envy. This didn't last long. Ricardo impregnated my mother and suddenly left Mongolia, never to be seen again. Abandoned by the first man she surrendered her body to, my mother became depressed and died shortly after giving birth to me. Before she died, she insisted that my name should be Od, to distance my destiny from the darkness that tinted hers.

All the people I knew called me Od.

I was raised by Arban, my grandfather who loved me, and also by Nekhii, my grandmother whose treatment of me I interpreted as hatred because I was the tragic memory of a departed daughter who took her years to conceive.

Under the eyes of my grandfather, who loved to tell stories of the desert, great rivers and mountains, my childhood prevailed over the sprawling capital of Mongolia. Beginning with the outer reaches of Ulaanbaatar where we lived, my eyes became familiar with the Gobi Desert at the extreme south. At the end of each month, I would leave Ulaanbaatar early in the morning to accompany my grandfather, who dealt in horse trading, to Dalandzadgad. After the end of our four-day stay in Dalandzadgad, as we prepared to return to Ulaanbaatar, my grandfather would have me look at the Gobi Desert as far as my eyes could go, until I was lost in its fathomless body that lapped the edges of Mongolia.

"I can't see anything, grandfather," I told Arban.

"There's always something to see when you look hard, son. Nothing is truly hidden," Arban said. "Have you ever seen a bent iron?"

"I have seen one before," I answered.

"The fact that an iron bends means it has a place for weakness. You'll never know unless you keep hitting at it. Look again," Arban ordered.

This time around I looked as hard as I could and saw nothing. Just when I was about to take my eyes away, I noticed something like a man running through the desert. I screamed, "Look, grandfather!"

"What do you see?" Arban asked.

"I see a man on a horse!" I shouted.

"See? You would not have seen him if you hadn't looked well. Nothing is truly hidden, you hear, Od?"

"Yes, Grandfather."

"Men are always so fortified that they reveal nothing but the cracks in the walls. Always remember this, son," Arban said.

As a child, I was always amazed by the waves of sands that sat on the deserts of Mongolia like a brown skin ready to clothe whoever passed through it with thirst and mortality. I told my grandfather this.

"To conquer the desert, become like the desert," my grandfather would say.

"How's that, Grandfather?" I asked Arban, not knowing that someday I would enter the desert and become part of it, forever defined by its taste and intent.

My grandfather's answer came like a prophecy. "Someday you'll understand, my boy," he said, patting my shoulders.

Arban and I continued the ritual of passing through the desert from when I was nine years old until my eleventh birthday when my life suddenly took a turn that would alter the course of my destiny forever.

I had begun to take notice of my grandmother's treatment of me at a tender age. She had always avoided me and whenever she spoke to me, she would raise her voice loud in anger, as if I was many miles away from her. One day in February after my childhood friend, Terbish, and I finished playing in the circle around the large compound, I sat in my grandfather's chair and watched my grandmother walking towards me, smiling at me for the first time in many years.

"Will you go with me to Mandalgovi tomorrow?" she asked me. She didn't wait for me to answer when she added, "I want you to come." Then she left me again.

The next day, I was all dressed and as soon as Nekhii came out from the room, my grandfather and I began to walk out of the house. When we reached outside of the house, Arban said, "Be back with the boy as soon as you can, Nekhii."

"I will," my grandmother answered.

I ran to Arban, kissed his forehead and followed my grandmother out. I had been to Mandalgovi many times before. My grandfather had always spoken about Mandalgovi whenever we passed through it on route to Dalandzadgad for horse-trading.

"It was where I met Nekhii," he would say with a dreamy look in his eyes as he relived his history. "She was the finest woman I ever laid my eyes on, Od," he added, clasping my hands as we rode on towards Dalandzadgad. One day, Arban stopped in the middle of the road, dismounted from the horse and took my face in his palms. When he spoke, his voice became more sober than his usual self, as if what he was about to say had more importance than every other thing he had ever told me.

"Your grandmother is a very good woman, you hear?"

"Yes, Grandfather," I answered.

"Tragedy can change any man. Your mother's death changed your grandmother and I am sorry that she hasn't been strong enough to love you as she should. But she loves you, you hear?"

"Yes, Grandfather," I answered again.

"Good! Let's go!" He helped me mount the horse again while we rode towards Dalandzadgad.

When we reached Mandalgovi Market, Nekhii and I stopped at the first shop. A tall, stern-looking man with piercing eyes emerged from it and began to walk in our direction. The moment he reached our side, he greeted Nekhii, gave her something wrapped in a leather bag and stood silently. Nekhii turned to me, took me aside and spoke.

"Od, you will go ahead with this man to get something for me. He is an acquaintance of your grandfather. Once you have collected it, he will bring you back here. My age does not allow me to walk around as much I would love to," my grandmother said.

"Okay, Grandmother. I will go with him." Immediately when I said this, I noticed that the face of the stern-looking man dissolved into a generous smile.

"Now go," Nekhii said. The strange man took my hand and just as we took a few steps away from her, my grandmother's voice stopped us.

"Wait." We waited.

Nekhii walked over to us, took my face in her palms exactly the way Arban did to me on the way to Dalandzadgad, and said, smiling, "I love you, Od."

"I love you, too, Grandmother," I said as I melted into her opened arms.

"Go," she ordered. I offered my hand to the stranger again and began to walk away from her. When I turned to see if she was still standing where we left her, I could see her wiping her face with the back of her hand. Nekhii had been crying. What was wrong? I was just going to collect something for her and the stranger will bring me back to her. I was coming back to her. I was coming back to Arban, to the stories of the mountains and the rivers and the great desert. Why was she crying as if I were walking into some great darkness that I might never return from again? I began to smile. Grandfather was right— Nekhii, my grandmother, had always loved me.

Now I believed.

CHAPTER TWO

Eating Dust

The stranger and I kept riding on horseback for what seemed like an eternity until we arrived at Baruunsuu, a village very close to Dalandzadgad. I had stopped with Arban several times here to water our horses, and I recognized the village.

"We are far away from Mandalgovi. This is the village of Baruunsuu," I said to the stranger. "When are we going back to my grandmother? It is getting late."

"You know your geography very well," I heard the stranger speak for the first time. His voice was even more menacing than his looks.

"Arban took me everywhere," I said.

"Who is Arban?" the stranger asked.

"My grandfather," I answered. Suddenly, I remembered Nekhii saying that the stranger was an acquaintance of my grandfather. I suspected foul play.

"Wait. My grandmother said you know Arban. Why would you ask me who Arban is? You don't know him, do you?"

The stranger gave a loud and evil laugh.

"I didn't know him before you mentioned his name."

"Let me down!" I screamed and began to struggle on the horse's back. By now, we were almost at the outskirts of Baruunsuu. Behind us, the only thing that could be seen was the dust kicked up by the hoofs of our horse.

"I'm sorry I can't, lad," the stranger said. Even at eleven years old, I had the strength of a teenager. I continued to struggle, and just when I was about to dismount, the stranger sent a blow to my face that made me lay flat on the horse, as if prostrating. Before I could regain my senses, I heard the stranger whistle. As if from nowhere, four other men emerged riding on horseback, each rider with a boy or a girl sitting in front of him. They rode in a circle, whistling in celebration until the stranger began to ride towards Agaruut, another small village that slept just a breath away from the great desert. The rest of the men followed his lead.

We camped in Agaruut.

At night, when I noticed that some of the men were not watching, a full-haired and soft-spoken girl called Altantsetseg, her younger sister named Chinua, another boy who I later came to know as Khulan, and I made a mad dash for our lives. We had no plans whatsoever for our escape. We just decided to try on impulse.

The men didn't waste time. They immediately heard our footsteps and raised an alarm. Soon we were heading back into the camp, Khulan limping on his right leg due to the hard kick one of the men gave him. That night we were taken into a cage and fed little food. I went to sleep dreaming of Arban holding my face in his palms as he said, "Your grandmother loves you, Od," and my grandmother holding my face in her palms as she said, "I love you, Od."

As soon as it was sunup, the men roused us to continue the journey. All the while, I remembered Arban's words that "Nothing is truly hidden" and I began to watch the movement of each of our captors like a hawk. Agaruut was the last place we passed through that I knew by name. After that, I had no idea where we were or where we were heading. I surrendered my destiny to uncertainty.

Early in the morning, we rode for a long time until we were out of Agaruut. At the mouth of the desert, two men and another girl sitting on one of the men's horses were waiting for our captors to join them. The moment we reached them, one of the men raised his right fist into the air, gave a loud salutation and the men in our train chorused in answer. He came down from his horse, lifted the girl off from its saddle and brought her to our cage. The girl and I held each other's eyes until the stranger who collected me from my grandmother opened the cage for the new rider to throw her inside. By now, we had totaled ten kidnapped children inside the cage, seven girls and three boys.

Together with the new rider, we continued to ride across empty spaces towards a vast collection of sands that disappeared into the mountain ranges. The mysteriously dusty taste of the desert air surrounded us with the smallest particles that attacked our eyes, even though we were inside a cage. The men had covered their faces and we could hardly see what they looked like. When the sun had risen to its highest, they stopped us a few times during the journey to give us water. After this, they counted us one by one.

Hours later, we had gone deep into the desert. Although we were in the same cage, none of us could say a word for fear of being punished by the man watching over us. It was only when the men had gathered all of us to take a rest that we had the opportunity to talk to each for the first time.

But no one spoke.

I spoke first and, in hushed tones, told the group about my plans for escape. I told them about my fears, how I had heard stories like ours before, and how if we did nothing, we would end up having our lives destroyed before our very eyes through slavery and prostitution. I knew this because I had once heard Arban speaking in Dalandzadgad with a horse trader whose daughter went missing for seven years. When she returned home, she brought nothing for him but a body covered in scars and stories of blood, starvation and attempted suicide. I did not tell my companions this. I simply lied to them and said I had watched a movie about it.

"Where will we go when we escape?" Jullian, one of the other boys, asked as he stared at my face.

"I heard one of the men saying there's a town nearby. We will go there. It is where the sun sets, Jullian. When you run, run towards it, you hear?" I said.

"Okay," Jullian replied.

I looked at the other children around me. Although none of them said anything, I could see clearly in their eyes that the thoughts of home excited them. As we prepared our escape, something happened that night which told me I needed to say there because it was right after it that I discovered how serious our captors were, even to the point of murder.

The night we escaped, we were five in number: Altantsetseg, Chinua, Khulan, Yuna and I. Jullian refused to come with us. When we began to run, I was ahead of the group, with Yuna following right behind me. Often, I turned back to see the others' progress. Altantsetseg and her sister, Chinua, were lagging behind. They held hands while running and when I turned back to Yuna, I realized that she was trying her best to defy the constraints of her age—eight years old—to make it. I kept shouting at her to keep running. She did.

Jullian must have given our captors the direction we took because soon enough, I heard the voices of the men not too far from us. They were in pursuit of us. I knew there was no way they could come after us using horses. They had been trying to maintain the horses for the remainder of the journey to wherever our destination was. I could remember that the day after we left Agaruut, one of the horses collapsed on the sand and refused to move.

Just when I had raised my voice to encourage Altantsetseg and Chinua to run faster, I heard the first gunshot. We needed to separate, and quickly, too. The men had seen us. I ran faster, climbed a heap of sand and waited for Yuna who was right behind me. Once she had reached me, I told her to run down the heap and never stop running, no matter what. She climbed the heap, held my hands, turned and in that great darkness that washed over the sands of the Gobi Desert, Yuna held my eyes with hers and as if she was making an attempt to speak, whispered to me, "I will see you someday, Od." With that, she quickly let go and began running without turning back.

When Yuna had left, there was another gunshot. This was the second time, and it was then I noticed that all this while, I hadn't seen Khulan. Remembering that he was still in pains from the injuries he had during out last escape attempt, I immediately turned and began running back, past Altantsetseg and Chinua, who were stunned to see me going back. Our captors were still wandering in the desert, although not too far from us. Because we were running on sands, there was no way they could hear the sound of our feet.

"Keep running!" I said to Altantsetseg and Chinua, who were already too tired.

"Where are you going, Od?" Chinua asked.

"Khulan... I'm going to get him!" I said.

"We left him behind; he's limping," Altantsetseg explained.

"See there?" I said, pointing east, "run in that direction. We must not run in the same direction. Yuna has gone down there already," I said again, pointing north where Yuna had disappeared behind the heaps of sand, hopefully to safety.

Altantsetseg and Chinua didn't move an inch.

"Go!" I commanded.

"I'm afraid," Altantsetseg confessed.

I took her hands before I spoke. "Look, I'm coming right behind you. Now go!"

I watched the two sisters as they ran in the eastern direction. Immediately, I started to run to Khulan. I met him lying on the ground, crying.

"Od, Od, Od," he called as soon as he saw me. In front of us, the fire from our captors' makeshift torches was closer.

"I'm here, Khulan," I said comfortingly. "Can you run?"

"No, no, Od. My legs... I can't," Khulan cried.

"Come...I will help you up," I offered. I bent down and once I had Khulan's arms around my shoulders, I lifted him.

We didn't go far when Khulan slumped on the ground again. I bent down to pick him when I noticed the blood dripping from the right side of his stomach. It became apparent that he had been shot by one of the bullets the men had fired. I heard him speak, his voice very faint.

"Yuna, Altantsetseg and Chinua... do you think they will make it?" Khulan asked.

"I hope so," I said. I watched him. I grew up with Arban and Nekhii as an only child. I had never had the presence of any other sibling around the house with me. The only person I had a close attachment to as a brother was my childhood friend, Terbish. Watching Khulan that day, Khulan who, along with Chinua, was just seven years old and the youngest among us, I felt broken and afraid that I was about to lose a brother.

"Go, Od. If you take me with you, I will slow you down. They...the men...they will catch you...see?" Khulan struggled to speak.

"If you see them, shoot them," I heard the voices say as they came closer to us.

"Go, Od," Khulan said. He smiled and added, "I will be fine."

I stood up. I knew that Altantsetseg and Chinua would not make any progress without me.

I saw our captors approaching and began to run. When I had gotten far enough from Khulan, I turned back. The men were already at his side. I saw one of them raise his gun and aim it downward.

'No! No! *Zogs!* No! *Uuchlaarai!*" It was Khulan, begging in Mongolian for his life. "No! No! Stop! No! Sorry!"

I closed my eyes.

"*Gal!*" one of the men ordered. "*Fire!*"

The gunshot echoed. A loud scream wrenched the silence of the great desert and then I opened my eyes, letting the tears drop. I ran away, crying. One of the men must have seen me, because I heard someone scream, "There! Follow!"

To this day, I still do not know how or where I got the strength to run the way I did that day as I headed east. I gave the men enough distance that it didn't take me long to reach Altantsetseg and Chinua, who had been running all this while and turned to see if I were following them.

"Run!" I screamed, so angry with them I could rip them apart. Had they seen what had happened to Khulan, they would not have waited for me to yell at them to run.

Altantsetseg and Chinua did not ask questions. They ran. Behind us, the men were catching up and I was already giving up when I remembered the words that Arban uttered that day in Dalandzadgad:

To conquer the desert, become like the desert.

I looked around me. Everywhere, there were holes dug in the deserts. I remembered stories that Arban told me about mammals and reptiles who would normally escape impending danger by digging holes in the sand to hide themselves. I asked Altantsetseg and Chinua to stop running.

"Did you hear the last gunshot?" I asked them.

"Yes," the two sisters chorused faintly. They looked so exhausted that if we continued running, one of them was bound to collapse on the sands.

"That was Khulan. He's dead. It was bad...very bad." I watched the sisters as I said this. I wanted them to be afraid, and when they gasped, I knew that they were.

"Do you want to live?" I asked.

"Yes," they chorused again.

"Good. You must do whatever I ask you to do."

I took Altantsetseg's hands and explained my plans to her. Hurriedly, I expanded one of the holes, put Chinua inside and told her to cover her nose with her palms while I began to cover her with sand, leaving her head partly in the open.

Once I was done with Chinua, I repeated the process with Altantsetseg. When I had made sure they could not be seen, I turned in the direction of the heap I made Yuna go down and ran to it. When I reached the heap, I stopped running and lay flat on my stomach. Even in this position, I could see clearly as three of the men arrived at the place I had hidden Altantsetseg and Chinua.

"They must have left," I heard the man with the gun say.

"No, I am sure they are somewhere around here. How is it possible for four little kids to just disappear out in the desert?" It was the stranger who took me from Nekhii at the market in Mandalgovi.

"Who are you asking?" asked the man with the gun. "It is that boy you brought. I knew he was trouble right from the first time he attempted to escape."

"Are you blaming me for your negligence? Were you not supposed to be watching over them? Fucking drunk!" the stranger cursed.

"What did you just call me?" the man with the gun asked.

"Fucking..."

The man with the gun didn't wait for the stranger to finish when he sent him to the ground with a bullet. I silently prayed that neither of the girls would scream out of panic. From the look of the two remaining men, it seemed the girls did not. The man with the gun went to the stranger he just shot, searched his pockets and retrieved what must be the Mongolian Tugrik. A minute later, I watched as the two men turned and began to walk back to the camp. I let them get a safe distance away before I left the heap and ran to Altantsetseg and Chinua. I reached the holes, pulled them out of the sand and dusted them off. I went to the dead stranger and found a small jar of water in his bag. I drank a little and gave it to Altantsetseg and Chinua. Once the girls were done drinking, I spoke to them.

"We need to continue running. If we are lucky, we may find a friendly face or place."

"Okay," the girls answered. By now, they had surrendered their safety to my hands. We began to run east. None of us looked back as we went deeper into the desert, but as I ran thought of Yuna. Had she gotten to safety? Was she alive? What's happening to her now?

I was thinking of Yuna when I heard a gunshot and a voice rising into the air.

"Stop or I'll shoot!"

Altantsetseg, Chinua and I stopped dead in our tracks. I raised my head slowly and saw another group of kidnappers with their train. We had escaped our captors only to land right into the nest of other kidnappers.

CHAPTER THREE

Not Yet...

Two wagons pulled over to us as we froze in our spot, fear written on our faces. Chinua began to cry. I put my arms around her and told her to keep quiet, we would be fine. Two men, one of them a large, broad-shouldered man with a turbaned head and another who was the exact opposite of his companion, came down from the first wagon.

"What are three little children doing in the middle of the desert at this time of the night?" the heavily-built man asked. He did not wait for us to speak before he concluded, "I guess you three must have escaped from your masters, right?"

"No, sir," Altantsetseg replied.

The smaller man pulled a pistol from his pocket and pointed it at us. The image of Khulan being shot rushed into my mind.

"Forgive us, sir," I pleaded. "Yes, we escaped our masters."

"I see," the heavily-built man said, turning to his companion. "Manga, what should we do with them?"

Even in the dark, the little light from the men's torch had shown Manga coiling his lips as he grinned wickedly at us. He was still holding his gun.

"You kids have three options," Manga said, drawing closer to Altantsetseg. He put his hands through her hair and then began to trace her body with his fingertips. "One, we take you back to your masters. I am quite sure they must still be looking for you. Oh, what they would do to you!" Manga left Altantsetseg and drew closer to Chinua, who fidgeted and melted into her sister's arms. Manga didn't mind. He did with her what he had done with Altantsetseg. Tracing his fingertips through her hair, he gave his second option. "Two, you come with us." He left Chinua and came to my side. He pulled his gun and placed it on my forehead. "Finally, I shoot all of you and leave you little devils to rot in the middle of the desert. Now, choose before I make the decision for you."

The two sisters turned to me. I knew that if I said we should be taken back to our captors, the men would not agree to that. And I also knew that they would rather have us killed than to take us back. I decided that it was better to stay alive.

"We will go with you," I told Manga.

Clap! Clap! Clap!

It was the broad-shouldered man who I later got to know as Nugai. He was obviously the one in charge of this kidnapping train.

"Great choice, lad," he said, patting me on the shoulders. "Manga, get them into the cage. And blindfold them. I don't trust them at all," he glanced at me, "especially the boy."

A few minutes later, Manga tied our hands and bundled us into a cage that, apparently, had other children within our age group. We were blindfolded as the horses pulled the wagons to another unknown destination.

I had no idea how many days we had been going through the desert. All around me, it was pure darkness. I could see nothing except what was going on inside of me. It would be dishonest to say I did not think of Yuna and Arban all the while. I wondered what my grandfather must be going through now without me. I wondered what excuses Nekhii must have given him to explain what happened to me. It was a collection of dark nights that created storms in my heart.

We kept going through the desert. Just when I had heard the wagon stop and had thought that we must have reached our destination, I heard the screams of a girl in the other cage.

"Get her out! Get her out right now," a man barked.

Two or three torches must have come to life because soon I was able to see through my blindfold as the men ran to the other wagon. A man went into the cage, untied the screaming girl's hands, opened the door, and took off her blindfold as he shoved her outside the cage violently. Her feet hit the sands as she slumped backward, weakly.

"Leave her there and let's go!" the same man barked again.

I never knew what had caused the girl to scream. As our wagon drove away, I became grateful for the blindfold, happy that I could not see the girl abandoned in the desert while her captors continued their journey.

I felt someone touch me and wondered who it was. Even though I could not see anyone in the cage, I knew there were many of us inside, probably about eleven.

"Altantsetseg, is that you?" I asked.

"Shhh..." Altantsetseg silenced me. "Don't cry, Od."

I closed my eyes and thought of Arban, my grandfather who had loved me long before I knew what the world was or what it would do to me.

And then I wept.

CHAPTER FOUR

Partitions

The caravan stopped, and the men ushered us out of our cages. There were several of us, but we were not allowed to talk to anyone. One of the girls with us had been bowing her head, refusing to look at anyone's face. I took special notice of her, out of curiosity. Although she was probably around Yuna's age, she was taller than Yuna and had a large mass of hair that spiraled down to her shoulders more than Altantsetseg's hair did on hers. I made sure I stay close to Altantsetseg and Chinua so that we would not be separated.

I observed my environment from where I stood with the rest of the children. We were in a small town right in the underbelly of the China-

Mongolia border and here was where our kidnappers would partition each of their captives. It was from here that each captive's fate would rest on surviving the dangerous world that we had been forced into.

There were men and women moving about the place, selling food, clothing, guns, drugs, cooking oil and humans. There were also police men with amenable characters talking with the captors as if they were long-term friends who were seeing each other for the first time in years. I turned back to the other children. Like me, the look on their faces betrayed their ignorance. It would be years before I learned that many of them didn't know that we had just crossed the border into China, and some of us, unless we were lucky, would never see our parents or our homes again.

We were ushered into a concrete-walled building where a man and woman sat atop a chair in the far side of the room. Immediately when they saw us, the woman, who wore a carefully-painted face and dressed in blue and gold, rose to her feet and walked to Nugai.

"Oh, Nugai! It's been quite some time. I feared you'd decided not to come today," the woman said.

"Have I ever broken my promises?" Nugai asked. "Business is good. Some of them, their parents were far more cooperative than I'd imagined they would be, but I had to be a bit more persuasive with some of the parents. Business is good, Nomin."

"That's great to know!" Nomin said. "Are these some of my babies?" She pointed at the girls who were lined up by Manga. Altantsetseg and Chinua stood right beside me. I whispered to Altantsetseg to squeeze her face angrily throughout the duration of the session. Chinua must have heard me, too, because she made the same facial expression. My thought was that if we were to be sold, no one would be ready to buy an angry person.

When Nomin saw me, her smiling face became distorted. She was apparently not expecting a boy in her party, since I was the only male among the children brought by Nugai and Manga.

"What's he doing here?" Nomin asked Nugai.

"We found him and these two girls in the desert," Nugai explained, pointing at Altantsetseg and Chinua. "The boy looks like trouble. He escaped from his initial captors. Don't worry, he's not for you. Someone will find a world for him here in China."

"I will take him," a voice said in the most impeccable English I had ever heard to that point.

It belonged to the man sitting with Nomin. He was so lanky that it seemed even standing straight stole all his energy. The man smiled as he looked at me, as if to weigh how much trouble I could be. He looked genuinely friendly, despite his line of business.

"Bat Erdene," Nomin called the man's name. "You are not staying long in China. You will be going back to Bangkok any moment now. Don't you think the boy will be too much trouble for you?"

"I'm still around and will have the boy, Nomin," Bat Erdene said. "And that's final!"

"Yes, sir," Nomin and Nugai answered simultaneously. Bat Erdene began to walk out of the room with such fluidity that he appeared weightless. Coupled with his beard and white moustache, his movement was nothing short of regality and intimidation. All this while, I had been intrigued by the way Nomin and Nugai fidgeted in Bat Erdene's presence. I had a feeling he must be a prominent and feared man. I hacked up a plan that needed to be acted upon, now.

"Sir," I called out, stepping forward. When Bat Erdene stopped, I fell on my knees and began to cry. I pointed at Altantsetseg and Chinua, who had begun to cry before I did. The mere thought of me separating from them must have hit them very hard; a morbid fear was written all over their faces.

"I was taken from home with my two sisters—Altantsetseg and Chinua—and my brother, Khulan. Khulan... he is not here.... He was shot in the desert and I... I left him to die, sir. Please, if you take me, also take my sisters with you. Don't keep us far from each other. They are already broken, sir. Please. Please. I will do anything." By now, I was already at Bar Erdene's feet while speaking. I was crying in between.

Bat Erdene walked over to Altantsetseg and Chinua and walked his hands through the girls' long, cascading hair in the same way that Manga did when they found us in the desert. Once he was done inspecting the girls, Bat Erdene sighed and turned to Nomin.

"Have them washed, Nomin. I will come back in an hour."

"Yes, sir," Nomin replied.

"Oh! I almost forgot," Bat Erdene said. He walked over to the girl who had refused to look up at anyone. "What is your name, beautiful girl?"

"Qara," the girl answered.

"Qara, you are coming with me, too," Bat Erdene said as he began to leave the room. He motioned to Nugai, who rushed to him. "Come with me. These are your wares. Let me know how much you are taking for each of them, especially the boy!"

Just when Bat Erdene had opened the curtains to the outside world that slept in the underbelly of the China-Mongolia border, his voice came rushing into the room:

"Make sure they bathe, Nomin. They smell like pigs!"

***

I wasn't concerned about the fact that we were blindfolded and tied up again in the back of a Bat Erdene's wagon as we left Nomin's place. I was more worried about the choice I had made by letting Altantsetseg and Chinua come along with me. I wondered if I had made the right choice, if Bat Erdene would treat them well. The wagon was speeding along the road as if it were using borrowed tires. We were tossed from side to side, our heads crashing against the walls of the car. I knew there were four of us in the back of the wagon. Because Altantsetseg and Chinua had always loved to stay right beside me, I reached out my right hand and took Altantsetseg's hand, just to let her know I was still around and that everything would be okay. She withdrew her hand. I took it again.

"It's Qara," Qara said.

"I'm sorry," I said and took back my hand.

Qara didn't say anything. Few minutes later, as the wagon kept pushing the road backward, I felt a hand melting with mine. It was Qara's.

For the first time in many days, I fell asleep.

CHAPTER FIVE

The Beginning of Dark Days

We lived in the dark in China. Our presence in Zhengzhou, the capital city of Henan Province, was kept as secretive as possible. The building we lived in was a story edifice that belonged to Bat Erdene. It was built in a way that those inside the building could see the streets but those on the streets could not see inside the building.

It was night when we first arrived there. The van pulled into the drive and, soon, I could feel the blindfold slipping down my face. Once I got used to the lights around me and I could see clearly, I turned to make sure that Altantsetseg and Chinua were with me. They were, Altantsetseg smiling painfully at me when our eyes met. She took her sister's hand protectively and walked up to me. I raised my eyes to see an old man, possibly in his late sixties or early seventies, open the gate for us. His name was Ming. I turned my gaze away immediately when Ming caught me looking at him. I would later get to know that everywhere that Bat Erdene went to, he took Ming with him and that Ming had been with him for more than twenty years. Bat Erdene treated the old man with the utmost respect, and I wondered if Ming knew the line of his boss' business or if he was just casting a blind eye to it. Ming continued to look at the ground until Bat Erdene opened the car door and went to greet him. They communicated in perfect English. While Bat Erdene and the old man talked, his body guard, a huge Chinese man called Zheng, came over to our door and opened it.

"Follow me," he said.

Altantsetseg, Chinua, Qara and I followed Zheng into the large house. The house had a narrow pathway with small rooms on each side. I counted about twenty-eight rooms on the first floor of the house alone. Each room had a curtain that was transparent from the inside and lighted by a bulb that gave out little rays of blue light. There was also a bed in each room with a table on both sides and a wardrobe attached to the wall. I later discovered that most of the girls that came with us that day and others that we met in the house were mainly from the countryside of Mongolia, Myanmar, Taiwan, North Korea, Romania, Kazakhstan, and Thailand. Others were taken on the premise of receiving a better education in China. Most of the girls who fell in this category were the ones we met when we first came. They were sophisticated and more adept at handling people that came in and out of the building.

This night would be the first night that Altantsetseg, Chinua and I would finally be separated. The moment that Zheng showed a room to Altantsetseg and told her to go in, she took Chinua by the hand and began to walk into the room with her.

"What do you think you are doing?" Zheng asked.

"I don't understand," Altantsetseg replied, visibly surprised and afraid at the same time.

"Leave her. You go in alone. She has her own room," Zheng said, taking Chinua's hand away.

Chinua freed herself from the huge man's grip and ran to her sister, hugging her tightly. Zheng had had enough. He began to walk to towards the girl furiously and I was afraid that he might hurt Altantsetseg and Chinua and there was nothing I could do. Our lives had not only begun to change, but we had no idea how much it would change what we were forever. None of the new arrivals knew what we had landed into. It would take only a few days, especially for some of the girls who were wise and discerning, to know their current fate. As a boy amongst a vast collection of girls of different nationalities, I was practically left at the mercy of Bat Erdene, who had still not found time for me.

Just when I thought that Zheng would strike either Altantsetseg or Chinua in the face, a voice came from the hallway that stopped the huge man's hand midway.

"The little girl can put up with her sister for today only, can she not, Zheng?" Bat Erdene said, looking at Zheng directly in the eyes with his trademark smile. It seemed it was only Bar Erdene that could calm his bodyguard's short temper and did so only when it became necessary for him.

"If you say so, Bat Erdene," Zheng replied.

"Then let it be so."

Once Bat Erdene felt that he had settled with Zheng, he walked over to Altantsetseg and Chinua, retrieved a small knife from his pocket and dangled it in front of Chinua's face.

"What's this, my angel?" he asked.

Chinua said nothing.

"What is this?" Bat Erdene shouted.

"A knife," Chinua answered.

"Good girl," Bat Erdene said, rubbing Chinua's hair. "Today will be the last time you sleep in your sister's room. If you ever create drama like this again, this knife will be for your sister's head. Understand?"

"Yes," Chinua answered, shivering. Bat Erdene stood up and looked at me.

"You, follow me," he said. I turned to look at Altantsetseg and Chinua, who had melted into her sister's arms. While I followed Bat Erdene, I stole glances at them, Altantsetseg watching me leaving until I disappeared out of sight.

CHAPTER SIX

The Things We Became

Bat Erdene entered a bedroom decorated with modern furniture. He slumped into one of the chairs and looked at me carefully, like one inspecting a commodity at the market, weighing whether to buy or not. Once he was satisfied, he beckoned me to be closer to him. I did.

"My beautiful boy," he said, taking my hands. He began to rub my hands the way Arban did when I was still very young. He moved to my face, rubbing it, then my hair and then suddenly put his index fingers into my mouth. I moved back, gagging.

"Get back here," Bat Erdene said. I could see that he was furious. I moved closer to him.

Immediately, he put the same finger into my mouth again.

"Lick it," he ordered. I was afraid of him. I began to lick his fingers. Bat Erdene moaned into my fingers, almost sleepily. Whenever I stopped, he would snap into consciousness and would then order me to continue. After what seemed like an eternity, he finally removed his fingers, smiling.

"You will do just fine, boy," he said. "I wanted to taste the water before swimming in it. It is my philosophy, you know. Do you know what philosophy is?"

"No, sir," I answered.

"Ah, poor boy. You will know that someday," he comforted, as if it were a great loss not to know what philosophy was.

"I will take care of you, I promise. But you must do whatever I need you to do. Do we have a deal?" he asked.

Even though I didn't understand what he meant then when he said "deal," I knew that Bat Erdene must be a dangerous man who would go to any length to get whatever he wanted and at any cost. I nodded.

"Now that we have a deal, uhhm...." Bat Erdene stopped and pointed at me. "What's that your name again?"

"Od," I answered.

"Fine name. My wife used to love the stars, you know. She's dead now," he said.

"I'm sorry sir," I apologized for lack of anything better to say.

"No, don't be. I killed her!" Bat Erdene said and burst into a wild laugh, as if to imitate the ghost of his wife. "But never mind. As I was saying, now that we have a deal, I trust you to keep your end of it. If you ever try to escape from this place, I will find you and, before your very eyes, I will shoot one of those girls you have been trying to protect. Don't play hero here. Don't be too dramatic here. You are too young for that shit."

I was still standing before Bat Erdene even as he spoke. I watched as he stood up, removed his shirt, went to a wardrobe, threw it inside and came back to the spinning chair at the reading table. He leaned back on it, the light illuminating his face and white hair. He looked relaxed as he smiled at me. Turning around in the swivel chair with force, the chair spinning, Bat Erdene stood up again, removed his trousers, then his boxers and in a matter of seconds, he was naked before me.

All my life, I had never seen a naked adult before. The only person who had seen my nakedness and whose nakedness I had also seen was my childhood friend, Terbish. When I saw Bat Erdene naked, his manhood dangling as he moved around the room, saying nothing but looking at me, I turned to leave the room. His voice stopped me.

"You will sleep here tonight, boy, and many other nights to come. You belong to me now," Bat Erdene said. He ordered, "Say what I just said!"

"What, sir?" I asked.

"'You belong to me now'," he repeated.

"I belong to you now," I answered.

"Good boy!" I could see Bat Erdene was excited. "Come here!"

I took a few steps him. He ordered me to come closer and I did.

"Undress," he said.

"Sir?" I asked. No matter how hard I tried not to look at Bat Erdene, I could not help myself looking up to see his straight face as he looked me. He chuckled at my embarrassed face and walked over to me, telling me to raise my hands up. I did.

I was still as he pulled my shirt off my body. I didn't know how long I was standing in the middle of the room, but soon enough, I was naked and Bat Erdene was naked, too, standing before me, looking into my face, smiling. Unsure of how to react, I began to move away again and just like before, Bat Erdene's voice stopped me again.

"Go into the bathroom. We are going to have a bath, you and I."

His voice suspended in midair, as if he was finding it difficult to breathe. I had no idea which of the rooms in the bedroom led to the bathroom, so I continued to stand until Bat Erdene came over, took my hands and let me into the bathroom. Once we were inside, he shut the door, and suddenly pushed me backward, forcefully. As my head banged against the tiled walls, I let a loud scream. At the same moment, I heard Bat Erdene laughing wildly, as if he were a child playing a game.

I wished Arban was there with me. He would have taken me, Altantsetseg, Chinua and Qara out of there. But Arban was not there. And as the tears swelled in my eyes, partially blinding me from seeing Bat Erdene's hairy face coming close to my face, then kissing my forehead, while his hands reached down to my thighs, I remembered Nekhii telling me "I love you, Od," and for the first time in my life, I cursed my grandmother's name.

CHAPTER SEVEN

Zheng

The next morning, I didn't wish to see what I saw when I opened my eyes. I was lying on the floor in blood, my foot in between the rope that tied my hands together. Bat Erdene woke me with a kick and ordered me to go and wash up my body in the bathroom. I did. By the time I was through cleaning myself in the bathroom, Bat Erdene was dressed. I came out, took my clothes, and began to follow him out of the room.

"Where are you going?" Bat Erdene asked.

"Outside," I answered weakly.

"No need to go outside. You will stay in this room until I tell you to go outside," Bat Erdene answered, walking back into the room. He took my hands as he spoke.

"Have you any idea what favour I was doing you the moment I agreed to take you in? Look at this building. Each girl in this building has a room to herself. In some places, there are four or five girls in a single room. Look at the life I have given you and your sisters. All I need you to do is to stay here, do what I need you to do and respect me. Failure to do so is to end your life and that of those miserable girls you call sisters." I watched Bat Erdene moving about the room like an enraged animal and I became afraid of what he might do to either Altantsetseg or Chinua, or both of them. I retreated further into the room.

"Good boy," Bat Erdene said, going to the door. Before he went out, he turned back and glared at me one more time.

"By the way, who the hell is Yuna? You don't go calling random names each night when you are with me boy, or I will have that untamed tongue cut off!" Bat Erdene said and banged the door closed behind him. I waited until I heard the keys turning and his footsteps fading away before I gave out a loud cry. I wasn't the only one giving a loud cry each night. Sometimes, whenever I listened very well, I could hear loud cries coming out from the other rooms where some of the girls were kept. I didn't need to be told the reason why. I knew. I wondered if the voices belong to Altantsetseg, Chinua or Qara. I wondered if Yuna, if she were alive and wherever she was, cried like the girls and I did, too.

Later, I picked myself up from the floor, went to the window and drew the curtains aside. I could see the streets from the window, the people moving about their businesses, none of them, perhaps, aware of the things that were going on behind the white mansion. Years later, when I had spent time enough time in Zhengzhou, I got to know that the locals respected and feared Bat Erdene as they had known him and his generosity to them for more than a decade. Maybe they knew his activities and, like Ming, they had decided to turn a blind eye to them.

I was still at the window looking at the streets when I felt as if someone were watching me. I was right. When I looked towards the gate, I could see Ming looking up at me. This time around, I didn't turn my face away but held his eyes until he disappeared out of sight.

The window became my only contact with the outside world. It was from there that I was able to observe the influx of people into the compound, mostly in the evenings. They came in expensive cars. Like the girls who came from different countries, the men, too, were Chinese, Russians, Mongolians, Taiwanese, and so on. I did not need to be told. These men were all wealthy and that must be what had set Bat Erdene apart and made him even more powerful: he drew his clients in from the powerhouse of society.

And at night, Bat Erdene would tie me up and have his way with me. In the morning, he would lock the door and not return until the evening. In the mornings and afternoons, someone always came to open the door and pass a plate of food and water to me then lock the door again. I never saw the person's face, but I suspected it was Zheng. He was the only one that Bat Erdene could trust to put fear in me. The two men thought me fearless and Bat Erdene said this every night while flogging me, first in the bathroom and then in the bedroom, until he saw my skin turn to red.

I spent the next year and a half in Zhengzhou living that same way. In truth, I had lost track of time. I had become so in tuned with my thoughts that nothing else interested me. I still had thoughts of Arban, Yuna, Altantsetseg, Chinua and Qara, thoughts that were even more potent than they were a year ago.

In a strange twist of fate, my sessions with Bat Erdene had gone beyond sex. My English was far better than when I had left home. Bat Erdene would talk to me, and whenever I responded in a way he did not like, he would go into a rage before correcting me. It was also through him that I had come to learn a lot about human nature. I watched Bat Erdene intently, studying him, since he was the only human I was in contact with the entire year.

I was changing fast, accepting my fate. The only thing that made me realize who I was and that one day I might leave this place was that I had not forgotten Arban, Yuna, Altantsetseg, Chinua and Qara. I wondered what was happening to all the people I had come to love since fate had brought us together.

I still called Yuna's name at night. I didn't know when I did that, but Bat Erdene would whip me, complaining that I still called out strange names. One day, he asked me who Yuna was, and I told him she was my mom.

I had not seen Altantsetseg, Chinua, or Qara since the day that we were separated. Some days, I would stand by the window and watch Ming as he watched me until he disappeared from sight.

One day, I was standing by the window when I heard voices coming from downstairs. A minute later, I saw more than twenty-six girls pouring into the compound, led by a fat woman whose face I could not see clearly. The mere thought of seeing Altantsetseg, Chinua, Qara, or any of them excited me so much that, for the first time, I forgot I was a hostage. I stood by the window, watching each girl going towards the gate. Ming still looked at me intermittently.

I did not see Altantsetseg, Chinua or Qara. Just when I was about to give up, I saw a girl with a long mass of hair walking slowly to the gate. It was Altantsetseg! But where was Chinua? As if to answer me, she emerged, walking slowly like her sister. They were no longer holding hands, these two sisters who could not afford to be a split second away from each other, who ran through the desert inseparable. What had Zhengzhou done to Altantsetseg and Chinua?

The fat lady gave a curse and went back into the house. Few minutes later, she came out, dragging a girl along.

It was Qara!

Even as Qara was being pulled violently by the woman, her head was still down. When they reached the gate, the fat lady went out first, and just when she was about to walk through, Qara raised her head and looked up at the window. Our eyes met. She was the first person to do that since the day I was thrown into Bat Erdene's room. She did not stop looking at me until a hand reached through the gate and pulled her out. Ming closed the gate and then, turning to me, waved at the window for the first time then quickly moved away, as if not to be caught.

I retreated from the window and went to the mirror to look at myself. From what I had seen from the window, Altantsetseg, Chinua and Qara had changed physically. They were looking bigger, as if they had transformed into women overnight, and they had the moment that their childhood, like mine, was stolen from them. I stared at myself in the mirror. I still had my curly hair and pointed nose. I had also gained some weight.

Bat Erdene had not been in the room for a week by that point. Many months later when he returned, I was set free into a world of sex, rape and drugs.

...Two Years Later

It was during my second year that I began to gradually emerge into Bat Erdene's world. By then, I was already thirteen but had the body and strength of a sixteen-year old. Bat Erdene did not give me full exposure to the public nor independence until something occurred which made him not only release me but also grant some of the girls major room to breathe.

One evening, a week before Bat Erdene's scheduled return from Thailand, I was in the room when Zheng suddenly opened the door and peeped inside.

"Bathe," he said and threw some new sets of clothes into the room.

I went into the bathroom and had my bath. When I came into the room, I was surprised to see Zheng still inside. I went to the chair and sat down without looking at him.

"Dress up in this," Zheng said, pointing to the cloths.

Realizing that he was not leaving the room any time soon, I forgot about him, stood up and removed my trousers. Zheng glared at me until I was completely naked. I went to the flow and picked up the clothes he brought. When I was fully dressed, he stood up and told me to wait. I watched as he went out and then a few minutes later, he returned with a white man. The man's hands went into his pocket and soon reappeared with a twenty-dollar note which he gave to Zheng. Zheng, smiling, came to where I was standing close to the bed.

"Do whatever he tells you to do," he said. "He's Bat Erdene's man, you hear?"

"Yes," I answered.

Zheng disappeared from the room. The white man drew close to me and began to inspect me like a prized horse. I stood motionless, already used to this. That evening would be the first time that another man other than Bat Erdene touched my body.

By the time I was done with the white man, it was already dark. He removed his wallet, retrieved a hundred-dollar bill and gave it to me. I collected it, not knowing what to do with it. Something in my mind told me I would have a need for it someday. When the white man left, I did not dress immediately; instead, I slumped on the ground and fell asleep. It was early in the morning when I heard the door doorknob turning and I woke up. When the sleep cleared fully from my eyes, I saw Bat Erdene smiling at me. I felt nothing when I saw him. He came over and patted me. Then, raising his left hand, he offered me a vase of snapdragon flowers.

"For you," he said, his face still entertaining a smile. "My wife loved flowers."

I collected the flowers from him and placed them on the table. Bat Erdene was sniffing the room like a dog. His eyes were red with anger in a way that I never saw in him before.

"Od, was someone in this room when I was away?" he asked.

I saw no need to lie to Bat Erdene. I opened my mouth and let the truth spill out like water. "Yes, Bat Erdene," I said. "A white man was here. Zheng brought him in. He said he's your man."

"He's my man? He's my man? He's not my fucking man!" Bat Erdene screamed. "I have to teach that bastard a final lesson." Before I could say anything, I heard the door bang, and the door locked again. Bat Erdene was out.

I began to pace the room. I had never seen Bat Erdene act that way. I had a feeling he was out to do something terrible to Zheng. I did not know how long Zheng had been in Bat Erdene's service, but I knew whatever it was that was between them was a purely master-servant relationship, and Zheng, like all those who worked for Bat Erdene, was afraid of the man as if his life depended on that one thing—fear. My feelings were right. Five minutes after Bat Erdene left the room, I heard a gunshot. I went to the door and tried to open it. It was locked. I could hear the frantic voices of people moving in and out of the house. Someone had definitely been shot and I knew who it was-Zheng.

I remembered the window and dashed toward it, waiting. Soon, I saw four hefty men that I had begun to see with Bat Erdene in the weeks before he travelled to Thailand carrying a dead body to a car. It was Zheng's.

Five minutes later, I heard the doorknob turning again. I sprang away from the window toward the middle of the room just as Bat Erdene opened the door and entered. His anger was gone. In its place was a smile that he wore as if to show he was satisfied with whatever it was he had just done. He said nothing to me. He was simply a man satisfied with the fact he had no need to explain his cruelty. He went over to the bed and fell upon it, the smile still pasted on his face.

The next morning when I woke up, Bat Erdene was gone. This went on until the day another major event occurred.

CHAPTER EIGHT

A Flower for Qara

I had spent close to three years without seeing Altantsetseg, Chinua and Qara except through the window. At the end of every month, the girls would line up and leave the house for what I later discovered to be a medical check-up, to see which of them had gotten an infection, especially HIV or other STIs. I always looked forward to this; it was the only time that I was able to see Altantsetseg, Chinua and Qara. Qara still put her head down whenever she walked, and I noticed that she had begun to walk very unusually. Her movements were slow and seemed to take a lot of energy from her. She was becoming frailer. She must have told Altantsetseg and Chinua that I stood at the window. Whenever they went out, Altantsetseg,

Chinua and Qara would all look up at the window and wave at me. I noticed that the three girls and I were not the only ones who used to smile whenever that happened. Ming, too, would participate in the act, as if it were a conspiracy that he was ready to indulge himself in, despite his age. I was grateful for him. It seemed to me that he and I had forged a bond. Each day that I stood by the window, Ming would come out to the gate just to look at me and then he would wave before disappearing.

One early morning, when I was in bed with Bat Erdene, it was the loud screams of a woman that woke the house up. Bat Erdene sprang out of bed and, drawing his pants up his thighs, hurriedly left the room without locking it. I weighed whether this was my time to see other people fully or to wait inside until Bat Erdene returned. I still remember the rage in his eyes that led him to kill

Zheng. Finally, I decided to go out. For the first time in the three years since I arrived in China, I opened the door to the room by myself, took the stairs to the first floor and began to walk through the hallway. I saw no one. When I passed the first few rooms, Chinua, who must be twelve years old by now and already grown up, ran to me. She hugged me deeply and without saying a single word, she took my hand and let me into a room.

There, hanging on the rope midway between the ceiling and the floor, was the reason for the scream that morning. Qara's head was looking down while her tongue spilled out of her mouth, loosely, as if to mock the entire universe in death. Her large mass of hair fell from her head and covered her face. Chinua was still holding my hand. I removed my hand from her grip and without looking back, climbed the stairs, weakly, back to Bat Erdene's room.

When I entered the room, I began to cry. I went to the wall and bashed my head against it. Why did she have to die like that, hanging like a common criminal? Where did she get the rope from? I kept asking myself these questions as I paced the room. Suddenly, I heard noises again.

I went to the window and saw a car drive through the large gate. Two of Bat Erdene's hefty men, the same men who took Zheng's body to the car the night he was killed, came out from the mansion with Qara's body. Her head was still facing down. I stood by the window until Qara's body was driven out of the compound. A few minutes later, Bat Erdene came into the room and saw where I was sitting. He hesitated before he closed the door and came fully into the room.

"A girl... a girl was sick. She fainted. That's why you heard that scream," Bat Erdene explained. It was obvious he had no idea I went downstairs. When he noticed that I was not about to say anything, he sighed, went to the wardrobe, picked some items that I didn't see and left the room. Through the window, I saw Bat Erdene being driven out of the compound. They must have gone out to follow Qara's body wherever it was they were taking her. I peeled my eyes away from the window and suddenly saw the snapdragon flowers that Bat Erdene had brought. I went over to the flowers, took them, and came back to the window. I began to pull the flowers one by one, dropping them to the ground. With each flower that I dropped, I called Qara's name, imagining her taking my hands in the back of Bat Erdene's wagon three years ago. It was the first and last time that Qara and I had ever spoken to each other.

Ming, as usual, was looking up at me as I dropped the snapdragon flowers from the window. When our eyes met, he clasped his hands together and kowtowed. I waved at him and moved away from the window.

Bat Erdene didn't return to the house that night. I slept alone. In the middle of the night, I dreamed that Khulan was lying in the desert calling my name "Od, Od" and just when I was about to reach him, he shouted "No! No! *Zogs!* No! *Uuchlaarai!*" before the bullet tore him to pieces.

The image suddenly turned to Qara. Qara and I were running in a street in Zhengzhou. I was far ahead of her when she called "Od, wait for me!" Just when I turned back to see how far she was from me, I saw her body hanging in the air, her face laughing at the dust.

Then, the image evolved, back to four years ago in Ulaanbaatar: Arban and I were riding a horse through the great desert when suddenly I turned to see only his horse behind me. Arban was on the sand calling my name and before I could reach him, the desert rose and covered my grandfather with sands.

The last image I saw in my dream that night was of Yuna. We were standing on top of a heap in the middle of the desert when she suddenly fell and began to cry, "Od, help me!" I turned back swiftly, just in time to find her in the hands of a woman, her body drenched in blood that poured out of her thighs.

Although I was too young to be sensational about my dreams, I thought that there was a possibility that Arban was dead and that Yuna had been caught by another woman and was subjected to the same life that Altantsetseg and Chinua were living in Zhengzhou.

The following morning, I was asleep when Bat Erdene walked into the room and woke me up.

"I am leaving for Bangkok. You will come with me, you and your sisters."

"When do we leave?" I asked. I was grateful that I did not need to ask him if we could bring Altantsetseg and Chinua along with us.

"We leave tomorrow evening. If I were alone, I would go by air. The train intersects at Zhengzhou. We will take the night train from there to Bangkok. It's a two-day journey. I need to warn you again. I don't want you to go playing the hero. I don't waste time killing a man. I have been doing that all my life. Like I told you few years ago when you first came here, if you try anything stupid, I shall not hesitate to shoot you, Altantsetseg, Chinua or all of you. I bought you with my money not for business but for my personal pleasures. Without me, you'd have been rotting in the mines or on the streets by now. For the last time, I don't want you to go playing the hero. What did I say?" Bat Erdene asked.

"No playing hero," I replied.

"Good summary!" said Bat Erdene. "You can go and meet your sisters now."

"Yes, Bat Erdene," I answered and left the room.

I found Altantsetseg downstairs, sitting alone. She mumbled something when she heard movement; her eyes barely opened.

"Altantsetseg," I called. Immediately when she heard my voice, she sprang to life. She stood up and hugged me and then quickly withdrew from my body, as if something shocked her. I understood.

I felt the same thing, too, when she hugged me. I had not been touched for three years by anyone apart from Bat Erdene and the one time Chinua hugged me and held my hands, the day that Qara died. Altantsetseg's embrace felt strange to me, but I loved it. I took her hand as I spoke.

"Where's Chinua?" I asked.

"She's in her room, Od. She has changed," Altantsetseg replied.

"What do you mean she has changed?"

"She's into drugs now. She stays in her room all day staring at the walls, calling our parents' names." Altantsetseg began to cry as she spoke. "I tried, Od. All these years, I tried to keep her safe. But, look, we have all changed. You have changed. I have changed. Qara is gone and the future is just so bleak for everyone here. How did we get here? What did we do wrong?" Altantsetseg's tears flowed uncontrollably. I did the only thing that came naturally to me. I took her into my arms and held her. I was silent until she had cried enough and then suddenly extricated herself out of my arms. I was surprised. It was when she withdrew from me that I noticed one of her cheeks was unusually swelled up.

"Altantsetseg, what happened to you?" I asked.

"Nothing, Od. It's business as usual," she said.

"No, I have never seen you like this before," I said. "Don't hide a thing from me. What happened to you?"

"Chai was here," Altantsetseg confessed, turning her face to the wall.

"What did he want?" I asked.

Bat Erdene had made it clear that he did not want any of the men working for him to have anything to do with the girls working for him. No man was to enter another girl's room unless their designated duty warranted them to do so.

When I asked Altantsetseg again what Chai was doing in her room, she told me the whole story. Chai had come in last night just after her last customer for the night was through with her. She was not apprehensive at first, but this did not last long. She became afraid the moment she saw that Chai had stayed in the room without saying anything to her. It was the look in his eyes that told her everything. She knew that look whenever she saw it, and she had seen it on different men that had walked through her thighs in the past. She asked Chai to leave. He didn't. Instead, he moved toward her, leering, as she moved back into the wall. Chai climbed the bed and hit her hard on the face. Even though she screamed, it was nearly impossible to hear her, due to the music that was coming from the bar. Chai went for her neck and squeezed it hard as if his intent was to make her choke. He didn't remove his hands until her eyes became round and her mouth parted, searching for breath. Immediately when Altantsetseg's legs were up in the air, Chai took the opportunity to pull them apart, so he could have his way with her. When it was all over, he quickly dismounted her and spoke for the first time.

"If anyone knows about this, you are dead!" After he said that, he went out of the room.

I didn't know how to react to Altantsetseg's rape. Although she had had sex with several men and had done so sometimes with men who loved it rough, she had done so willingly and expectantly because she had no choice. But to be forced into sex by a man who came to her when she was not willing and was not expectant, that was her breaking point.

"I am sorry to hear about this, Altantsetseg. I am sorry," I said

"I am so sorry, too," Altantsetseg apologized. "You have your own problems to worry about."

"No, I do not. I am alone. There is you and Chinua. You became my problem from the moment I was the only person that remained with you in the desert. I swore to be by your side the day that Khulan was shot before my eyes. I promise to find a way for you to return home, Altantsetseg," I said.

"Thank you, Od," Altantsetseg. "Do you think she is still alive?"

"Who?" I asked, genuinely confused by the sudden turn of the conversation.

"Yuna," Altantsetseg replied. "I always think of her."

"Me, too," I said. "I dreamed of her last night. I think she is alive."

"We are going away, Altantsetseg," I said, remembering what brought me out.

"To where?" Altantsetseg asked, searching my face.

"Bangkok, that's where Bat Erdene said. We leave tomorrow evening. I will go talk to Chinua. We are taking her along."

With that, I left Altantsetseg. I was about to go when I felt familiar eyes watching me. It was Ming's. I waved at the old man and began to walk back into the house. After three years of not seeing the outside world fully, I found little joy when I finally got the chance I had always wanted. The news of Chinua getting into drugs hurt me more than anything. I swore to myself that if the two sisters' lives were not any better in Bangkok, I would find a way to help them escape.

The next day, in the evening, Bat Erdene, his five hefty men, Ming, Altantsetseg, Chinua and I were on our way to Bangkok.

CHAPTER NINE

A Changing World

Bangkok was a bit kinder to me than China was. Bat Erdene gave me more space than he had done during the previous years I was with him in Zhengzhou. And unlike Zhengzhou, he had stopped coming to me for his sexual satisfaction. In Bangkok, he got a new boy to replace me. The only time any of us saw the boy was the day he was brought into the magnificent house we lived in Sukhumvit, a settlement thrown right into the heart of Bangkok's night life, hotels and popular restaurants. The house had a large field for parking cars and a hall that served as a bar where there were daily evening parties for the high and mighty of Bangkok. This was where some of the girls walked around the bar for the delight of some of the men, after which a girl would be taken for the night if a man saw her and liked her.

When we finally began selling Bat Erdene's drugs, we roamed the open and extensive streets of Sukhumvit which, according to the locals, led directly into neighboring Cambodia. The whisper around the house was that Bat Erdene's new sex toy was an eleven-year-old boy abducted from Colombia with his sister, who was dropped somewhere in Bangkok no one knew. Whether this story was true or not, I never knew. No one had ever seen the boy's sister or confirmed his nationality. No one knew the boy's name, either. He was simply called "The Beautiful." And we all agreed with Bat Erdene for naming him "The Beautiful" for he was truly beautiful and looked more girlish than any boy I had met before. Like The Beautiful, children, mostly girls within the ages of ten, eleven and twelve, were constantly brought into the house. Some of them spent a long time working for Bat Erdene until their teenage years while others were resold or sent out as soon as they came.

In Sukhumvit, Bat Erdene had begun to ask me about the things that happened each time he was away. He continued to go out into and outside Bangkok with his five hefty men. The most ruthless of them was Chai, Altantsetseg's rapist and a six-foot-plus tattooed menace. Chai had a long scar on his forehead that he tried to conceal by constantly wearing a black face cap, no matter his dressing or the time of day.

I had noticed that before we came to Sukhumvit, Bat Erdene was already having troubles trusting his men with confidential issues. This started to happen after he killed Zheng, who was the person he could most easily trust. As a result of this, he began to treat me with more kindness, putting some responsibilities on me each time he was travelling.

In the house in Sukhumvit, the girls were all expected to be in their rooms until they were allowed to go outside under the supervision of Bat Erdene's men. Their laughter, their quarrels, their play and every other thing they did outside their rooms were supervised by these men. One of my first major works for Bat Erdene was entering each girl's room to deliver food to her, the way Zheng used to do when I was Bat Erdene's sexual prisoner in China. But unlike Zheng, I was allowed to enter fully into the room and I could see the face of each girl I was serving. It was quite apparent that Bat Erdene's operation in Bangkok was different than the one in China, but something told me he was treating me this way so that, by entering each girl's room, I could hear and see what was happening and then report to him.

There was only one room I was not allowed to enter. Its entrance was through the east side of the mansion, which also happened to be the backyard of the house. It belonged to the Dancing Girl. Apart from the caretaker woman who attended to the girls, the only time any of Bat Erdene's men or I could see the pole-dancer was in the evening when she would come out to the bar to entertain the guests at the pole. The rumour was that she was a virgin and that she would remain so until Bat Erdene allowed any man to touch her. The Dancing Girl danced four times a week. She danced like a girl possessed and, sometimes, she would break out into the piercing cry of a manic. It was during those four days that the bar was filled to the brim. Her performances were looked forward by not only Bat Erdene's clients but also everyone who worked for him, especially Batu.

"She is magical!" Batu exclaimed. "Where did such a small girl learn how to dance like that?"

"Because she has magic, idiot," Chai fired.

Batu did not answer. Instead, he left Chai, who pulled out a cigarette and signaled me to light it. I did. When Chai talked, no one talked back. The only person he was said to be afraid of was Bat Erdene, but even Bat Erdene seemed afraid of Chai. They shared a mutual respect for each other's ruthlessness. No one knew anything about the night he raped Altantsetseg when we were in China. I still didn't know how, but I was sure that Chai was bound to pay for his sins soon.

I watched Chai smoke his cigarette. When he saw me looking at him, he extended the cigarette to me and said, "Smoke."

I declined.

"Come on! Be a man! Here, try it," Chai offered again. This time around, I took the cigarette from him and inhaled it. Even though I had lived with Bat Erdene all these years, I had never smoked before. I found this surprising because all the men in Bat Erdene's house smoked. Even the old man, Ming, was a chronic smoker, but he did not crack pot.

I did not inhale through the cigarette when I first took it. I just sucked some smoke in and held it in my mouth then blew it out. Even then, the air moving through my body felt hot, as if the whole of my body was on fire. When I breathed out, bouts of coughs escaped from me suddenly.

"Fuck! You are wasting it, kid!" Chai protested.

"Here," he said, taking the stick back to demonstrate, "try to just get each drag of this into your lungs and then try to breathe as if you are underwater. It means you don't breathe at all. You hold your breath, just a little, small. We good?"

"We are good. I will try that again," I said. This time around, I first inhaled through the cigarette and then I took it out and breathed out. As I took a few, extended draws of the cigarette and gently blew its smoke out of my mouth and nose, I found the feeling delightful.

"Good kid," Chai commended. "You will be good. The way you held the cigarette while talking to me, the way you look around you, your eyes moving about as if you are superior, you will be high, here," Chai demonstrated by raising his hands above us, "above the world. Just smoke well, kid, you will be fine." Chai began to walk away, and just before he disappeared from the bar, he turned to me and said again, "Don't kill yourself in the process, though."

All this while, I had no idea that the Dancing Girl had finished singing. It was when Chai had left that I turned to look at my environment and I caught her looking at me, disappointed. Chai's cigarette was still with me. I didn't know what to do with the butt. I wanted to kill off the embers and then look for a trashcan to drop it in but there was none close to me. I took my eyes off the Dancing Girl and stared at the cigarette again as it continued to burn. This time around, I brought it to my lips, looked at the Dancing Girl, and inhaled it deeply as I walked away from her watching eyes.

That day with Chai marked my initiation to smoking. I became a long-time smoker and I never looked back.

Although I was easily the kind of person to keep accounts of things happening around me, something I learned to do from Arban, I kept my distance from Bat Erdene, forever defining him as the man who had bought and treated me as a slave, defiled me and was now looking for me to trust him again. No matter how hard I tried, I could not forgive him and every day that passed by, I prayed for the opportunity to exact my vengeance on him. I didn't let Bat Erdene know this. I played it cool whenever he was around me. I was still his captive, with little freedom to move around.

CHAPTER TEN

CHINUA

Each little chance I got, I checked to see if Altantsetseg and Chinua were doing okay. The two sisters still pulled in the highest number of clients for Bat Erdene, especially Europeans and Americans, mostly expatriate workers in Bangkok. Sometimes I wondered if Altantsetseg and Chinua had forgotten about Qara. Since the day she died, Altantsetseg and I only spoke about her once, and that was the last day we were to leave Zhengzhou.

But we always spoke about Yuna, as if she were always there with us. I still remembered her. These days, I thought of her often, convinced that she was closer to me, physically, than all those years I spent without seeing her face. What would she look like? Would I remember her face when I finally got the chance to see her? Would she remember me? Would she remember my name? I didn't say any of this to Altantsetseg, of course, but they were my biggest worries.

I wanted Yuna to remember me as much as I hoped to remember her.

Once in a while, I thought of Arban, too. As the years passed, I had completely stopped thinking of my grandmother, Nekhii. I had a new life to live, and there was no way I could live it if I continued to think of how she betrayed and sold her own blood.

Chinua had changed. Although she had stopped taking drugs, she detached herself from all of us in Bat Erdene's house, including her sister, Altantsetseg. Altantsetseg, too, wasn't as bothered as she would have been years ago. She went on with her life. A few months after we arrived in

Bangkok, a certain middle-aged American man began to frequent the house and asked for no girl apart from Chinua. Whenever he came around, he would throw money at any girl he saw on the way as he was being led to Chinua's room. One day, I thought she was alone when I entered into the room with the pretense to give her food just so I could talk with her, but I saw the American man inside. I turned to go back when the man's voice stopped me.

"Hey, come here, boy," the man said.

I stood in the middle of the room and looked at the man. "Sir?"

"Take this," said the American and extended a hundred dollar note to me. I was looking at Chinua when the man was speaking. Her cheeks were red, as if all the blood in her body were there. I could see she was desperately mouthing something to me. I studied her lips, trying to make out what she was trying to say. When I couldn't, I shook my head.

"What? You don't like it, boy?" the American said, thinking that by shaking my head, I was rejecting his money. "This is dollars, boy. It's above your station, get it? Above your fucking country! No one says no to dollars. Now take it and get the shit out of my face!"

I collected the money and left the room. This was the second time that an American man had given money to me. I still had the hundred-dollar note from the saga that led to Zheng's killing two years ago in Zhengzhou. This made it two hundred-dollar notes.

The next day, I came to give food to Chinua when I noticed a new girl sitting on her bed. The girl could not have been more than fourteen years of age. When she saw me, she recoiled her legs back into her body and turned her face away from me. I did not speak to her. I dropped the plate of food and left the room to search for Altantsetseg. I met her alone in her room.

"Where is Chinua?" I asked immediately, a cigarette in my right hand.

"She's gone," Altantsetseg answered, staring at the wall. Although I had always been looking after Altantsetseg and her sister, I had stopped observing how much they had changed. Even though Chinua was thirteen years old, she could easily pass for eighteen. Her features had changed and her behaviour was no longer that of a child, yet I had always treated her like a child, a younger sister.

Altantsetseg, too, was not the same. The most visible change in her was facial. In place of her once smooth and soft cheeks was a hardness that gave her the looks of a girl already tired of life.

"What do you mean 'she's gone'?" I asked.

"Gone with the white man...she left late last night. She came to my room, told me she was going...that Jeremy, yes, that's the white man's name, has promised her marriage if only she could come with him. She came to say goodbye. Bat Erdene was there. She looked too sad for a bride. I asked her if she told you, she said she did. I couldn't stop her, Od. There was nothing I could do. I am sorry," Altantsetseg said and began to cry.

"She was mouthing something to me yesterday evening," I explained. "I couldn't understand."

Altantsetseg did not say anything. She was facing the wall, crying. I left the room.

None of us dared ask Bat Erdene what truly happened between Jeremy and Chinua or why he allowed her to leave. My guess was that he had sold Chinua away as a bride not to Jeremy himself but possibly a Chinese or Thai man. I had heard stories of marriages between abducted girls and the men from the countries they were taken to. I didn't tell Altantsetseg this. One day, she might have to find out the truth for herself.

Neither Altantsetseg nor I saw Chinua again. Like Qara, we gradually stopped speaking of her. Most nights, I couldn't sleep. I thought of everyone who had been with me that night in the desert, running for our lives. Khulan was dead. Chinua was gone. And now, I didn't know if Yuna was alive or dead. I had lost all of them except Altantsetseg. That night, I knew what I had to do.

CHAPTER ELEVEN

Saving Altantsetseg

Bangkok was the nerve center of Bat Erdene's illegal business. In China, I thought his only business was providing girls for the satisfaction of men. It was in Bangkok that I got to know how powerful he truly was. His illegal business included sourcing cocaine, heroin, MDMA and Methamphetamine from China and distributing them to some of the neighboring countries around Thailand. Even though he was protected by highly-placed individuals in the Thai police force, we were extremely careful not to be caught whenever we entered the streets of Bangkok to deliver our "packages." Most of our clients were gangsters, small drug dealers and junkies who received us in their houses. It was during one of these visits to sell Bat Erdene's goods that I found a way to set Altantsetseg free.

Ming and I had become friendly with each other. Bat Erdene's henchmen always followed us around whenever we went outside of the house into the streets of Bangkok to sell drugs. One Saturday morning, Ming stopped me.

"Are you good?" he asked, looking at me with concern.

"I am fine," I said.

"I have not been seeing the other girl," he said. Just then, Altantsetseg passed us at the gate with the other girls. Ming pointed at her direction and said, "The girl who used to hold this girl's hands back in China. I have not been seeing her. Is she still around?"

More than most occupants, Ming was the only person I was sure should be completely aware about the people who went in and out of Bat Erdene's house. I was genuinely surprised that he wasn't aware of Chinua's disappearance. This only meant that Bat Erdene and the American man had planned how to take her away from the residence without Ming's knowledge. I explained to Ming what had happened, speaking with such detachment that he would not be able to read my emotions. I told myself that I should not trust anyone, not even Ming, who was seen everybody in the house as a kind-hearted and gentle man trying to make a living.

No one around the house ever saw Ming as evil, but I knew what money could do. It was money that made my grandmother sell me into this life. Perhaps Bat Erdene, knowing how much I cared for both Altantsetseg and Chinua, had instigated Ming to find out something from me.

I began to be careful of Ming until two days later, in the evening, when I was moving around the house serving clients and some of the girls. Ming drew me aside again when he was sure no one was watching us.

"I have found a way to help the girl escape," Ming said, offering me a cigarette. When Ming smoked, he smoked like all old men did: in great contemplation of the universe and people around them.

"Which girl?" I asked, confused, even as I took the cigarette.

"The girl I showed you two days ago, Altantsetseg. Here, take this," he said, dropping a piece of paper into my hand. "Phichit will be expecting her today. That's his address. I know it's hard, but I want you to trust me, son," Ming said. I trusted him. Ming was partially the reason I was able to remember Arban all these years. His mannerisms and facial features were like those of my grandfather. I trusted Ming. I collected the piece of paper from him.

Southeast of Sukhumvit was Khlong Toei, a neighborhood which sharply contrasted with the opulence of Sukhumvit. From Khlong Toei, one could easily get to the Cambodian border. Whenever we went out to distribute Bat Erdene's drugs, some of us transferred our package to other kids and that was how the chain continued until the prospective client got their drugs. Few of Bat Erdene's captives were allowed to go beyond the Sukhumvit Road. We were watched on both sides of the road by his henchmen. We were watched from the top of big apartment high-rises, the Skytrain and the perpetual traffic jam. For each boy or girl (mostly girls) carrying a package, there was one man attached to them. Despite this, it was easy to escape after about a year of being watched. Once the men had seen that a girl or a boy always delivered a package and returned without any drama for ten months or about a year, they reduced their vigilance. This was usually the perfect time to try one's luck. A lot of victims who didn't know this had tried to escape before but were caught and shot dead. This was the only way Bat Erdene knew to instill fear into us.

None of us could see the faces of the men watching us. Even if we did, there was no way one could know if a smiling man that one passed on the road worked for Bat Erdene. Everyone seemed to work for him, from the policeman to the civilian on the street, from the rich to the poor. Here in Bangkok, Bat Erdene was highly regarded by the people as a philanthropist and by the politicians as one of the most powerful financiers of political ambitions.

According to Ming, one of the policemen that would be on duty at the BTS Sukhumvit Line was Phichit.

"He is honest, unlike the rest. If she was able to get Bat Erdene's men distracted, she could escape, find Phichit and he would take care of the rest."

"I trust you, Ming," I said. "Do you trust this 'Phichit' guy?"

"Let me tell you something, son. If I had had a way to take you away from here six years ago, I would have done so. I have been working for Bat Erdene for about two decades now and each day I live, I have regrets. Bat Erdene is one of the most dangerous men in Bangkok. He has killed so many before. He is ready to kill again and continue killing. My conscience is restless that I work for a man like that. And look at all the years I have been doing that! I am on old man. Phichit's father was my best friend. We roamed the streets of Sukhumvit as children during the last days of World War II. What you see before you today is not what was there decades ago. All of this was rice fields, boy. All of this, you get it? His father, good Anurak... yes, that's his name...he was a good man. Phichit is a good. His first daughter... Anong, she was kidnapped right before her mother's eyes. She was just eight years old. Where was Phichit? He was out there drinking with his friends, son. Yes! I remember this so clearly...like it was yesterday. He never saw his daughter again. He went deeper into liquor, drugs and women to save himself from being tormented by the memory of Anong. But, at last, he decided to do something. He joined the Thai police and swore to fight the system protecting the people behind trafficking in Bangkok. He has never looked back. So, do I trust Phichit? Yes, I trust him, just as I trusted his father. Trust me, boy, you have never seen such a good man before," Ming concluded and walked away from me. I wanted to go after the old man, thinking I had offended him with my question, when I saw Batu, one of Bat Erdene's henchmen coming. I retreated back into the house.

I was ready.

According to Ming, whenever Phichit helped anyone to escape from Bangkok to return home to Mongolia, he gave them the contact of a man in China that would see them through China right into Mongolia. If Altantsetseg could escape Bat Erdene's men, she could leave Bangkok by sunrise.

When I relayed my plan with Ming to Altantsetseg, she was extremely happy to return home. I was in her room that day to give her food. She ran to me and embraced me warmly. And then she was somber. It was typical of Altantsetseg to change her attitude at any time. I was already used to this side of her.

"What? What happen?" I asked.

"What about you? Are you coming with me?"

"No, I am not...even though I would love to go with you," I said. "It's better that only one of us go at a time."

Ming had warned that if anything went wrong, Bat Erdene would not hesitate to shoot all those he suspected. This was one of the many times that both Ming and Phichit would be helping victims to escape. They had never been caught or suspected. Bat Erdene trusted Ming and treated him as a father without knowing that his most trusted worker was actually one of the masterminds of the escape of his victims.

"I am afraid, Od," Altantsetseg said.

"I am afraid, too," I confessed. It was true. Altantsetseg was the last person I had. What if something happened to her? I could never forgive myself. "That is why I need you to be careful, Altantsetseg."

"I will," she said. She came to me and grabbed the cigarette that I was inhaling intermittently as we talked.

"I know I can't stop you from smoking, but I need you to try to stop," Altantsetseg said.

"I will," I said, careful not to make a promise to her. I had by now become so attached and dependent on cigarettes that I was unconsciously oblivious to it. I could remember days that I experienced bouts of withdrawal when I didn't smoke. I felt that by smoking, I had finally found a soft blanket and a way to escape my harsh place in Bat Erdene's world.

"Goodbye, Altantsetseg," I said and made to leave the room.

"Od," Altantsetseg called. I turned to her. She rushed to me. I opened my arms and swallowed her small frame, her mass of hair brushing my lips. This was Altantsetseg, sixteen years of age, and for the first time in six years, we would be going different ways, into whatever fate life had meted out to each of us. I was still as Altantsetseg withdrew from my arms. She looked at me with tears in her eyes. I left the room, and as I closed the door, her voice reached out to me, "Goodbye, Od."

That evening, we were out to distribute packages to clients as usual. The henchman who was attached to Altantsetseg was Batu. I was right beside him. Bat Erdene sometimes made me go with some of the girls right into the client's place and receive the money for the package delivered.

This did not always occur. Most clients prefer to wire the money into his bank account. But due to the fear of drawing suspicion to his line of business, Bat Erdene would rather collect the money in cash.

"Helps to keep the dogs away from sniffing your wealth, son," he would tell me, smiling. "You are doing just great! That is just what I wanted. But don't end up like Zheng," Bat Erdene would add as a subtle warning.

We were in the middle of Sukhumvit Road when I thought it was the right time to create a distraction. I scrutinized the people moving around and then picked as my victim a man coming in my direction, making a phone call. The moment I was an inch away from the man, I intentionally collided with him, and when his mobile phone, a Samsung that should be expensive, fell to the ground, I made as if to move backwards and then innocently stepped on it. As I had expected, it was all I needed to incense the man.

He barked at me, "You crazy? Dickhead!"

"You're crazy, too," I said. I wanted him to hit me first. He did. The moment his blow reached my face, I raised my fist high into the air and landed it on his face. Soon, passersby stopped moving to watch us. I could see some of the policemen running to the scene. But where was Batu, and Altantsetseg, too? I raised my eyes to see Batu talking to Altantsetseg then, leaving her behind, he rushed to where I was. Left alone, that was all Altantsetseg needed. My eyes went straight past Batu until I could see Altantsetseg had disappeared in the direction where Phichit would be waiting for her. Our plan had worked.

I was about to be handcuffed by a policeman when Batu reached my side. Immediately, he drew one of the police officers aside and spoke to him. The man came to me, dragged me away from the street and when everyone seemed to go on as if nothing had happened, he released me. It was when I was released that Batu realized we were actually without Altantsetseg. He turned around, scanning the people moving around. He saw no one. In order to not direct his suspicions to me, I joined him to search everywhere. Altantsetseg was nowhere to be found. Although my face showed I was worried, I was deeply happy that Altantsetseg was gone and, hopefully, safe.

Batu wanted to take his phone to dial a number, possibly to get one of Bat Erdene's henchmen to look out for Altantsetseg. Trying to buy her more time, I immediately told Batu we should search a bit, maybe we would find her. Batu agreed. We searched for Altantsetseg for about ten minutes before we finally gave up. By then, I knew I must have bought her enough time.

"Od," Batu called my name. I turned to him. From the first time I had met Batu, I had never seen him as fearful as he looked that day.

"Batu," I answered.

Batu was looking straight at the endless line of human bodies moving about in the busy Sukhumvit Road, looking as if he didn't hear me call his name. But I could hear his voice, a small whisper of his despair, "I am finished."

CHAPTER TWELVE

The End of The Beautiful

No one knew his name or if he truly came from Colombia. No one knew the name of the boy Bat Erdene called "The Beautiful" except me. We had already spent three years in Bangkok and the only time that any of the people inside the mansion saw him was the first day he was brought into the house. Because of this, he became a mystery to them.

Whenever Bat Erdene, who became busier when he returned to Bangkok, left the mansion early in the morning to foresee some of his several businesses, I would go into his room to give food to the boy. Unlike Zheng, who did not come fully into the room when I was Bat Erdene's sex pet, I always made sure that I entered the room. I wanted the boy to get used to me, to trust me. During the early days when I entered the room fully, he would roll the big blanket over his body, as if to protect himself from me. And whenever I caught him walking, he moved sleepily toward the bed, as if he could fall at any time. With time, he gradually got used to me. He had come to understand that whenever someone knocked, it would be me and no one else. Bat Erdene never knocked. He simply put the key in and opened the door.

One day, I came into the room to give The Beautiful food when I saw that he was naked. It was the first time I had seen him like this. When he turned his back to me, I noticed a long line of blood running through his bone marrow. I dropped the plate of food on the table and went to him. The moment I reached out my right hand to touch him, he screamed and moved away from me.

I sensed he thought I was trying to have sex with him.

"It's okay," I said, drawing away. "I won't touch you."

He was still panicked. He watched as I removed my shirt and then turned my back to him. He gasped. When I was sure he had seen the long stripes I had, too, I put on my shirt.

"He hurts me every day," The Beautiful said.

"I know," I replied. "You will be all right. I need you to be strong. I will get you out of here."

"How?" he asked.

"Because I can. I helped a girl called Altantsetseg escape. I will get you out of here, The Beautiful."

"Gabriel," the boy said.

"I don't understand."

"My name is Gabriel. My twin sister's name is Gabriella."

From that day forward, The Beautiful and I became close. Whenever I came into the room and Bat Erdene was not around, I would linger, talking with him. He would tell me everything about himself.

Altantsetseg had escaped for five days now. On the sixth day of her escape, Bat Erdene returned to the mansion. He had travelled to India to commission one of his many orphanages. Thirty minutes after his returned, I heard his voice outside the main compound, raised in anger. A moment later, Batu was knocking at my door. I came out and followed Batu to a patch at the eastern part of the house. Bat Erdene and all his henchmen were waiting for me there.

"Where did she go?" Bat Erdene asked the moment he saw me.

"Who, sir?" I asked, trying to make my face not to betray me.

"You know who I was asking about, damn you!" Bat Erdene shouted. "Now, where is Altantsetseg? I need an answer and I need it now!"

Altantsetseg was one of Bat Erdene's most popular girls and was more often demanded by men than any other girl he had. She had also sold more drugs than any other girl before. The only person that surpassed her accomplishments in the aspect of selling drugs was me, while Chinua came close to her in clients' demand for sex. Now he had sold off Chinua to someone in the name of marriage, thinking he still had one more sister to continue pulling in more clients.

"I have no idea, sir," I confessed. "After I was released by the Thai Policemen, Batu and I couldn't find her again. If she had planned an escape, she didn't tell me that, sir."

Bat Erdene slapped me hard on the cheeks. "You're still lying to me? Chai, get The Beautiful."

I was terrified. Had The Beautiful betrayed me? I had confessed to him that I helped Altantsetseg to escape and that I was ready to help him escape. I was deep in thought when Chai returned, dragging the boy.

"About six years ago, I warned you that the day you try to play hero would be the day that Altantsetseg's life, Chinua's life or yours would end," Bat Erdene said. "Now, thanks to you, there is no Altantsetseg here. There is no Chinua here, either. That leaves only you. And I can't end you now. I have some use for you. This means someone has to pay for you sins, doesn't it?"

I kept quiet.

"For the last time, where did she go?" Bat Erdene said.

"I don't know where..." I didn't know when Chai fired the gun on the order of Bat Erdene. I stopped speaking the moment I heard the piercing cry from The Beautiful, "Gabriella!!!"

I rushed to Gabriel. He was already dying. His voice was faint. While Bat Erdene and the rest of his henchmen were laughing, dismissive of the dying boy, I was able to pick his last words.

"Up there, Od. Up there. Gabriella. Up. She... up." And then there was silence. His index finger, flat on the ground, was pointing up. I looked up. Right above us, on the second storey of the mansion, was the Dancing Girl, looking down through the window. Unveiled, I could see her face, similar to that of The Beautiful Boy.

The Dancing Girl, who danced as if possessed by spirits, was Gabriella, Gabriel's sister.

I closed Gabriel's eyes and left the scene of the dead.

CHAPTER THIRTEEN

Some Dreams Come True

...Eleven Months Later

One evening, Bat Erdene called me into his room. Even after Gabriel's death, he continued to give me the same work I used to do, as if nothing happened, but I was already used to this side of him. Bat Erdene was the sort of man who could do an evil deed without a single moment of regret. Gabriella continued to dance at the bar, and her screams were becoming piercer than before.

"I am reselling some of the girls," Bat Erdene said the moment I entered the room. I stood at the door. He stood at the window, smoking as he spoke.

"Okay, sir," I said.

"New batches of girls are coming in from Chiang Rai. They were under the charge of my workers. One of the girls is a fucking murderer while the other has proven to be rebellious over the years, though she has calmed down a bit now." Bat Erdene paused and then, looking straight at me, he continued. "I am telling you not because you have the right to know. You are useful to me, and that is the only reason you are still alive or haven't been resold. I need you to behave. Any stupid move from you again, you are a goner! Did you hear me?"

"Yes, sir," I answered.

"You can go," Bat Erdene dismissed me.

I wondered why Bat Erdene would choose to tell me what he intended to do. Did he think that by telling me all these things, by drawing me into his confidence, he could make me become less stubborn than he believed I was?

Three days later, I came back from delivering a package and discovered that the new girls were due to arrive in an hour's time. I was eager to see them. I did not have to wait long. Thirty minutes after my return, Ming opened the gate to let in a black Mercedes. Two unconscious girls were taken from it into the house. My attention was drawn to one of the girls and as her head dangled in Chai's arms, I immediately knew who it was. After six years of being apart, after six years of me thinking she was dead, I was finally seeing her.

Yuna was alive and back again in the same place that I was. I had remembered Yuna. Would she remember me?

No matter how excited I was at seeing Yuna, I was careful not to let my emotions show. The moment that Bat Erdene or one of his henchmen discovered I was familiar with her, there was a chance that one of us would have to leave.

On the evening of their arrival, I was ready to serve the girls food. Because they were new arrivals, they were put in the same room, unlike in China when Altantsetseg and Chinua were almost separated the first day we arrived. When I entered the room, Yuna and the other girl were sitting on the bed talking. When they saw me, they kept quiet. At first, I was careful not to let the other girl know that I knew Yuna many years ago. When I remembered Bat Erdene saying that one of the girls was a murderer and the other a rebel, I knew that I was not meeting the usual kind of girl that I was used to all these years. I was meeting two who were almost as stubborn as I was, girls who were molested and raped but refused to be totally broken. In the few days I had known Yuna in the desert about six years ago, I had always suspected her to be so.

I dropped the food on the table for the girls without saying a word, and just when I was about to leave, I whispered, "Don't trust anyone, Yuna. Don't believe everything you see."

I knew that if I stayed for too long, Yuna or the other girl would try to talk to me. I left the room before either of them could say a word. There was only one thing I knew for sure. The moment I entered that room, I was convinced that Yuna remembered me. It showed in her expression. I went to my room and for the first time, I cried not out of sadness but happiness. I had always dreamed of the day that I would see her again, and I was glad it had finally come.

It was time I plan a way for both of us to finally leave Bat Erdene's world.

CHAPTER FOURTEEN

Happiness Mansion

One of the regular houses that we delivered packages to in Sukhumvit Road was called the Happiness Mansion. In stark irony to its name, Happiness Mansion was not really a mansion but a warehouse that could have passed for a Victorian pride. The massive structure was hidden within a realm of bars that were frequented by Western expatriates at Soi Cowboy in Soi 63, protected by a high roof and sharp archway windows. The mansion was originally built by a Thai millionaire as a warehouse for his toy and beads manufacturing business. The building, when it was almost at its completion stage, stopped when the millionaire was sent to jail for corruption and the building itself was claimed by the government.

That was more than twenty years ago, and Happiness Mansion was left exactly as it was, to the mercy of time.

It was said that there was not a single race that one couldn't find in Happiness Mansion, mostly a group of men and women of various ages that came together to make the building a home. Some stayed in Happiness Mansion for years while others simply lived there and once they had found their feet, they disappeared permanently into the streets to chase after the dreams they had dreamed of all their lives.

Inside the building, right from its stairs, one was welcomed by the stench and decay of some of the squatters' lives themselves. The smell could also come from unwashed clothes, toilets, tobacco, bread, cheese and other leftover food. Even though its owners, mostly men and a few women who were mostly drug dealers and prostitutes, belonged to the lower classes and their lives were from time to time haunted by poverty, they were known for their robust laughter and play that could easily be heard once one began to climb the stairs. This was the reason the mansion was called "Happiness Mansion" and was one of the most popular houses on Sukhumvit Road.

The dwellers of Happiness Mansion were also known to give generous tips to those who brought drugs to them. Some of them, who had not yet changed to the local money, would give a dollar to me. I was yet to spend the money I had been gathering since we came to Bangkok. Even then, I believed that someday I would have use for it. I got whatever I wanted from being at Bat Erdene's house. Bat Erdene had made it a principle not to give any of the children under him money, but he made sure that we were well fed and clothed. His reason was that if he gave money to people that he bought with his money, he would be empowering them to become rebellious and try to run away.

Not too far from Happiness Mansion was the collection of both locals and foreign sellers of fake Rolex watches and necklaces. At night, all these people poured into the roadside bars and pubs where they would, in turn, resell the drugs we sold to them.

I first came to Happiness Mansion with Altantsetseg about three years ago to give drugs to the occupants, who were mostly squatters without a real place to call home in Bangkok. I found the place so terrifying then that I stayed away from it as much as I could, but I was always sent back to it, and since I didn't have the right to make my own choices, I trained myself to get used to the occupants there. I observed their lives intently. There were always horrifying things going on in Happiness Mansion. Once, a Thai man who was in love with anything Western and had a nose ring put a gun to another squatter's head and began to ask for the return of something I was not aware of. When the other squatter dared him to pull the trigger, he did. A few minutes later, when I thought the whole incident would send the rest of the men into disarray, each man continued to do what he was doing as if nothing had happened.

All through the years I had known it, there were always people terrifying each other with knives, guns, or whatever they could find. Some were beaten, murdered, committed suicide, robbed, or driven into insanity; there was always someone returning from an institution, someone winding up at an institution; there were always girls in love with drug dealers; someone departing, someone arriving; there were always peace, war, danger, safety, comedy, tragedy, happiness, sadness, and through all these binaries, Happiness Mansion remained the same—a place they could always come to escape the uncertainties of a society that may never accept them again. It was here that they would come to "wait" until they would find their footing in life. Even though they fought with each other, they made sure that they protected one another whenever it became necessary. And out of this chaotic life, there was someone sane enough that was posted at the window to watch the cars driving by and the people passing through the street. This was mainly done for security reasons. Because there were a lot of people on Sukhumvit Road, one was bound to miss the cops unless one was vigilant enough to see them. That was mainly the duty of the man standing by the window.

I was frequently at Happiness Mansion until I became familiar with the men and women in it. Sometimes I came in the morning or afternoon and other times I came in the evening. Each of these times, I was bound to meet someone totally cracked up by drugs.

When I got used to them, the men loved me and personally reached out to tell Bat Erdene that they did not want any of his men in the mansion. All of his men, except me, whom they needed to bring drugs to them. Sometimes when I came, I would stick around for some time with the men until I was convinced that it was time to go.

Apart from drugs, the men were also in constant need of girls from Bat Erdene. This was why almost every girl who worked for Bat Erdene had been to Happiness Mansion.

This continued until my third year in Bangkok when I started taking Altantsetseg along with me. This was Bat Erdene's idea, since he felt that within the years, I had become busier than I used to be in previous years.

Exactly one year after Altantsetseg's departure from Bat Erdene's house and one month after the arrival of Yuna and Cyril, I saw Altantsetseg again at Happiness Mansion. Altantsetseg was back in Bangkok!

It happened like this:

One of the recognized occupants of Happiness Mansion was Li, a tattooed, bald, bearded Chinese man who had lived in the building for fifteen years. Even though he was just twenty-eight, he was not only feared and respected by all the other occupants but also by men of the Thai Police Force who were well acquainted with his history.

Word had it that when he was thirteen years old, Li and his elder brother, a drug dealer wanted by the Chinese police, fled China to Bangkok. Trying to keep a low profile, Cho took his younger brother and became one of the first occupants of

Happiness Mansion. But Cho's decision to keep a low profile didn't last long. Soon, he was swallowed by Bangkok's underground lifestyle. He went back to selling drugs and began to not only pull more occupants into Happiness mansion but also more police eyes, too.

In his second year in Bangkok, Cho was shot dead by, according to the police, a rival drug dealer whose name and face no one knew. Li was fifteen without a brother, a father, or a mother. With nowhere to go, he stayed behind in Bangkok and made Happiness Mansion a home, from which he began selling drugs at a faster speed than Cho did. By the time he was eighteen, he had lost count of the number of times he was in jail. It didn't take long for the police to stay off his trail as they believed that Li, who had witnessed his brother's death, believed that Cho was killed by the Thai police, and so he was always on the lookout for a reason to exact vengeance. Where Cho was straightforward and open in his dealing in drugs, the young Li was brutally secretive and cunning, so much so that the several times that the police tried to track him, he devised a means whereby nothing was found on him or in Happiness Mansion. With time, they partially gave up on him. Li was not doing drugs for the grandeur of money. He was doing it because it was the only thing that attached him to Cho and there was nothing the police could do about that. The other squatters, including those younger and older than him, respected him. Whenever he spoke, something he rarely did, he spoke loud and passionately.

Li was one of Bar Erdene's most popular customers on Sukhumvit Road. He had a special liking for me and I could never remember him calling me by my name. Instead, he chose to call me "My Boy." Even though he was not a person given to too much talk, he would always find one or two words to say to me whenever I delivered a package.

Shortly after he came back one evening from Chiang Rai, Bat Erdene called me and said he was sending me to Happiness Mansion to deliver a package for Li. Li had personally requested it. While I waited at the bar for Bat Erdene to call me for the package, I played cards with Batu in awkward silence. I had realized a long time ago that Batu had two feelings for me and nothing more than that: disgust and admiration. Batu was not happy that Bat Erdene treated me with consideration and, at the same time, Batu admired me for staying strong throughout these years, for rising to find favor in Bat Erdene's eyes. He told me so himself one day.

"Od, we never had a kid like you here before, you know," he said in a way that Bat Erdene himself would have spoken. By now, I knew that most people who worked and lived with Bat Erdene had his vocal mannerisms.

"Thank you, Batu," I said.

"But the day you decide to mess up, I will be the first to put a bullet through your fucking skull!" Batu said and disappeared.

Bat Erdene later called and within thirty minutes, I was climbing up the stairs that led to the large hall on the second floor of Happiness Mansion where the squatters hung around. Not all the people in the hall were squatters. Some of them would simply go there, smoke, drink, have conversations with their friends and then pick a woman to take home. There was always a woman for each man to take home.

When I entered the room, there was a woman with a great mass of hair sitting on Li's lap.

"My Boy," Li called the moment he saw me.

"Li," I answered. "I brought your package."

The moment I spoke, the woman turned her head and there, right there in the room, was the girl I had helped to escape Bangkok one year ago.

"Altantsetseg," I called.

"Od," she answered. She stood up and came to me, standing in front of me, torn between hugging me and not. I, too, did nothing. I couldn't believe Altantsetseg was back in Bangkok. *For how long*, I wondered. The tension in the room must have been thick because Li suddenly coughed and then spoke.

"She told me what happened, boy," he said. "You and I, including most of the people in this room, have all left home against our will. Life forced us to. You don't say anything anytime you are here. But you, My Boy, have always proved too smart for your age. Thank you for helping her escape, Od,"

Li concluded, calling my name for the first time since I knew him.

"Chai is still working for Bat Erdene," Li stated.

"He is," I said, wondering if I should have answered since Li didn't put it as a question. "Good."

I did not say anything. Altantsetseg was still standing before me.

"Go on, find a place and talk. I know you two need to," Li said.

Altantsetseg immediately took my hands and led me far away from the hall until we found an empty room.

"I am sorry," she said after it seemed I was not ready to talk first. It was all like a dream to me.

"He is dead," I said.

"Who, Od? Who is dead?" Altantsetseg asked, searching my face.

"Gabriel," I answered. "I killed him."

"Od, what are you saying? Can you just tell me everything?" Altantsetseg asked again, as if she were about to get angry.

"The Beautiful..." I began, speaking very slowly. "His name was Gabriel. The Dancing Girl was his twin sister. Her name is Gabriella. He and I...we were close...we were friends, good ones, Altantsetseg. I never knew how Bat Erdene knew since he was hardly around, but he knew. He also knew I helped you escape. I denied it. He insisted. When I denied again, that was when he asked Chai to bring the boy. I had thought Gabriel would tell Bat Erdene I helped you escape because I told him so, but he was brought for a different reason. Many years ago in China, Bat Erdene had warned me that the day I try to escape, he would shoot one of you. And if anyone of you escapes, someone must pay for it. I did not think of that. I did not! Bat Erdene asked me one last time where you were and when I said I didn't know, the gun went off, and Gabriel was lying on the ground, dying. He died in my arms, and the Dancing Girl was watching. She was at the window, watching helplessly as the boy she came into the world with left without her. You..." I said, pointing my index finger at Altantsetseg, "I killed the boy for you. I killed him. You have no right to be here. You have no fucking right!"

Altantsetseg had slumped on the tile floor and begun to cry. I didn't realize my eyes were wet until a tear dropped to the floor. This was the first time I spoke to anyone about Gabriel's death.

"I went home, Od," Altantsetseg's came like a whisper. "I went back to Mongolia. But I left again."

She had my attention now.

"Why did you come back?" I asked.

"I went home to my parents and told them what happened to me, to us, to me and Chinua and..." Altantsetseg stopped speaking.

"And what? Go on," I encouraged her.

"They told me I shouldn't have come back to Mongolia. I was no use to them the way I came back. And I had never been of use to them before. I packed my things and returned to Phuket. I worked there at several bars, and when I did not have enough money to sustain me, I decided to come back. I knew I could not go back to Bat Erdene. I came here. You know Li was always kind to us when we used to come here together," Altantsetseg said, her eyes teary.

"Why did your parents say what they said to you?" I asked.

"My parents sold my sister and me, Od," Altantsetseg said and began to try.

I went to her and embraced her. "I was sold by my grandmother, too. I discovered that the very first day we rode toward the desert with the stranger she sold me to. We were at Mandalgovi market when I was sold. You and I have been through a lot. I made a promise many years ago to myself. As long as Bat Erdene kept me alive, I would find a way to leave someday. I will find a way to make a life for myself. I hope you do the same, too. This is not the end of your life. Promise?" I held Altantsetseg's hands as I spoke.

"I will try to," she answered. Her answer was enough for me.

"No one will know you are here. Keep yourself safe and stay away from the streets," I said. I stood up and without looking back, I left Happiness Mansion. It was the last time that I would see Altantsetseg again.

CHAPTER FIFTEEN

Mapping a Way Out for Freedom

I told no one that I had seen Altantsetseg at Happiness Mansion. I was terrified that if Bat Erdene knew she was in Bangkok, he would do anything in his power to make sure she returned to him.

I still had plans to escape. Bat Erdene had stooges in all of the various Thai agencies in Bangkok and that was what made escape difficult for most of his victims. With the previous experiences I had, I knew that if I decided to take action, I had the support of Ming and Phichit, who were always willing and ready to be there beside me.

For the rest of my sixth year being with Bat Erdene, I became more immersed in his dealings in the underground world of selling drugs and subtly watching over the girls he had under his establishment.

I had not been speaking to Yuna. Whenever we happened to come across each other and there were people around us, especially Bat Erdene's henchmen, I would pretend I had never seen her before. Sometimes I wondered if Bat Erdene knew I knew Yuna. When I first met him during those years that I was his sex slave, he had always complained that I called a girl's name each night and the name was "Yuna". Had he connected me to Yuna yet? Or did he know but was testing me, to see what I would do? While I wondered about Bat Erdene, I also thought of what Yuna might think of my actions. Would she think I had completely changed to the extent that I was neglecting her?

One night when Gabriella, the Dancing Girl, was dancing at the bar and entertaining Bat Erdene's rich friends, I withdrew from the crowd and went to Ming's place. The old man was genuinely happy to see me. Since Gabriel's death, we had not really had time to talk again, and we always tried to be discreet, lest Bat Erdene or his henchmen began to take notice and suspect something was going on between us.

"Od," Ming began. "Good to see you."

"Good to see you, too, Ming," I replied. "You're good?"

"I should be asking you, kid," Ming said, smiling. "You're the one whose life is in another man's hand, to kill or to spare." Ming did not say this smiling.

"I want to leave someday, Ming," I confessed.

"You should. Who is stopping you now? Everyone you knew here is gone."

"No," I said.

"What do you mean?" Ming asked.

"There is still someone I need to take with me."

"Who would that be? You know you can't save everybody no matter how much you try, right?" Ming asked and offered me his cigarette.

"One of the new girls, Yuna," I said.

"What? Where did you know her?" Ming asked.

"We were captured together. We separated the day we decided to escape. Yuna was the first among us to escape from the kidnappers. I didn't know she was kidnapped again. All these years, I've been having nightmares that she might have been. I want to take her, Ming," I concluded.

Ming didn't say anything. He looked me straight in the face before he spoke again.

"Hey, kid, I know that look on your face. Yuna isn't the only person you are taking with you, right?"

"I still want to get Altantsetseg, too," I confessed.

"I see. Where will you go? Bat Erdene has eyes all over the city. I don't think Phichit can help all of you at the same time," Ming said.

"I don't know. I am still thinking about it."

"Good. Think carefully. The last time we saved someone, another died," Ming said, and his face became ashen.

"I am sorry to have dragged you into it, Ming," I pleaded.

"No, kid, I did what was right. And I will do it again."

I bade Ming goodbye. When we were able to meet again two days later, Ming was excited.

"Hey, kid, I know what you need to do when you finally get the girls," he said. He didn't wait for me to ask him when he outlined his plans for me.

Since Bat Erdene had men all over Bangkok, the only way possible for us to be safe after escaping was for us to run to an international embassy and present ourselves as victims of trafficking. According to Phichit, the Canadian Embassy would be willing to help us once they heard our story. He knew how he could get us there. Ming said he was surprised we didn't think of that a long time ago, but we freed ourselves of our ignorance by admitting that Bat Erdene had the hierarchy of the police force in his pocket, thus making us running to them futile.

Since I sometimes followed Yuna and Cyril on their deliveries, I felt that it was left to me to set a date and then we would attempt an escape. By now, the two girls had fully become Bat Erdene's girls and began to sell drugs for him, too. They would be dressed as Thai girls each time they went out to deliver a package in the morning or evening. That was not all they sold. Like all of Bat Erdene's girls, they were expected to make their bodies available to the clients upon request. That was why each girl was assigned a man who would wait outside the house for the time that said girl was inside the house. After she was done, she would meet the men where they would pick her and return her to the house. It was a regimented life, and most of Bat Erdene's henchmen followed this regiment to the letter. This was done so that she could not think of keeping any money she was given.

Most of the girls running errands for Bat Erdene were not aware that there were people attached to them. One only knew about this only if one was always observant enough to know. As a way to help the girls walk around the city, each of them was given a map until she knew the city by heart and would no longer had a need for the map.

I did not tell Yuna about my plans to help us escape. I thought it a wise thing to do due to what happened two days after my last meeting with Ming.

CHAPTER SIXTEEN

A Quiet World

It happened in the afternoon. I was standing on the balcony of the second floor of the house with Bat Erdene receiving orders from him when I saw Batu rush into the house, his shirt bloodied. Bat Erdene had also seen him and begun to come downstairs where we met Batu. Immediately he explained to us what happened. Chai had been shot dead! They were walking on Soi 23 when a bullet came from nowhere and seized Chai right in the forehead. He was shot twice and was dead in a second. Batu couldn't see where the bullets came from and he had no idea who would want Chai dead. Bat Erdene said nothing. He simply ordered Batu to go into the house and change. That was Bat Erdene. He knew that in his line of business, death, especially a violent one, was perceived as normal as drinking water.

Life continued as normal. Much of the time that I got to see Yuna was in the presence of other people, especially Bat Erdene, who had taken a special interest in her since the very first day she arrived.

Eleven months after the arrival of Yuna and Cyril into Bat Erdene's world, I felt it was time to make my move. I had waited for five of those months for Yuna to know the city by heart completely for fear that if we encountered problems with the initial plan, she would need to know how to navigate the city. My first plan was to go to Happiness Mansion and inform Altantsetseg so as to get her ready. This didn't work out as I had planned. Yuna met Altantsetseg before me and the moment Altantsetseg told her they were sold by their parents, Yuna lost it. She ran away from Happiness

Mansion, swearing never to return to Bat Erdene's place again.

The day she escaped and failed to return to the house, Bat Erdene was furious. The last time I saw him that way was the night he murdered Zheng in cold blood a few years ago in China.

He ordered a city-wide search for Yuna for four days and when none of his henchmen and some of the policemen on his payroll couldn't find her, he finally gave up on her.

One night, five days after Yuna's escape, Ming pulled me aside when Gabriella was dancing. Once Gabriella began to dance, neither Bat Erdene nor his men were fully aware of anything going on around them.

"I know where the girl is, kid," Ming said immediately we were out of earshot.

"What?" I exclaimed. "How?"

"I knew you would never get the chance to talk to her, so I did. I was able to convince her about Phichit. If any day she finally decides to leave, she should go to Phichit and tell him I sent her to him. She would stay with him for a week. After that, when the search for her is over, Phichit would know how to get her to the Canadian Embassy on Rama IV Road here in Bangkok."

I felt a deep sense of relief when Ming told me this. The day Yuna left, she seemed somewhat certain she knew where she was going. All along I was worried how she was going to make it out there alone. As soon as I learned that she was with Phichit, the burden was lifted off my shoulders.

For the first time in six years, I embraced Ming. When I disentangled from his body, he was looking at me affectionately.

"You were a kid when you first came here. And now just look at you, all big and trying to save the world," Ming said, laughing. "Go, see her, and find a way to get to Altantsetseg, too."

I left Ming.

The next morning, I went back to Happiness Mansion to talk to Altantsetseg and find out if she was ready to go with me. I found Li sitting alone in a room, smoking crack.

"My Boy," Li called the moment he saw me.

"Li," I answered. "I came to see Altantsetseg."

"You came too late. She left yesterday."

"Altantsetseg?" I asked, disorientated.

"You heard me. I couldn't stop her, you know. She said she is going to find her sister, Chinua. I have fucked a lot of girls, kid, but Altantsetseg? She crazy, kid, damaged. But I loved her. She should have stayed."

I began to walk out of the room.

"Chai is still working for Bat Erdene?" Li asked just when I was at the door. He had asked me this same question a year ago. I turned to see the simper on his face and I knew. Altantsetseg must have told Li what happened in China, the night that Chai raped her. It was then that everything fell into place. Li had either ordered the death of Chai or he had done it himself. I believed the latter. One of the stories about Li's fame as a killer was that few of his victims ever saw his face before he killed them. Didn't Batu say he didn't see the face of the killer? It was Li.

"He was," I said.

"Good to know. You are leaving," Li said as if he were accusing me.

"Yes, Li," I answered.

"Take care of yourself, kid," he said and bade me goodbye.

His voice followed me as I descended the stairs that led to his room.

"And fucking quit smoking!"

EPILOGUE

Goodbye, Ming

I found Yuna at Phichit's place. She had no idea that he was responsible for taking Altantsetseg back to Mongolia. It was the first time since she arrived in Bangkok that Yuna and I had had time to sit together and talk. She told me everything that had happened to her and her ordeal in the hands of Tuya, Xanadu and Hulagu. Although I had never met the three of them, I felt as if I were familiar with them since their names came up in most of Bat Erdene's conversations.

When Yuna had finished telling her story, I stood up and left her. I met Phichit sitting outside the house, as if on the lookout to make sure that I was not followed. He was a quiet man who did not say much. He looked to be probably in his forties but in his face, perhaps weighed down by the guilt caused by losing his daughter, Anong, he looked older.

Together, Phichit and I agreed that when the other girls and I escaped at night, a bus would be waiting just outside Bat Erdene's house to take us to another safe house close to the Canadian Embassy.

I bade Phichit goodbye.

Each night, Gabriella was made to dance for thirty minutes for the men at the bar. Once she was through, she would be led into her room by the woman who was the only person allowed into her room in the eastern part of the mansion. The plan was that once I could see Gabriella and convince her to follow me, Ming, who would be at the gate at that time, would give us a safe passage into the night. We had a firm belief that our plans would work since most of Bat Erdene's henchmen would not as vigilant as they would have been during the day. Their thinking was that most of the girls who would have thought of escaping would be busy with clients in their rooms.

We waited.

I would never know what happened that night or whose spirit decided to favour us. When Gabriella finished singing, I went to her as she was being led into her room by the other woman. I was hiding, waiting for the perfect moment to strike.

When they reached my side, I struck the woman with all my strength. She fell to the floor and lay down flat, unconscious. I dragged her into the room and pulled Gabriella in, quickly explaining my plot to her.

Gabriella and I came out of the room and found the passageway empty. That same night, Cyril, who I had told her of my plans earlier in the day, was alone in her room, waiting for us. I made the girls cover themselves with a veil as the three of us made our way out. The bar was still lively and I told the girls to wait. I went to Ming and once I had given them the signal, Cyril and Gabriella ran toward the gate. Ming opened it for the girls to go out first. They did.

I turned to Ming and with tears in my eyes, I embraced him. It was the only way I knew how to say "Thank you" to him.

"Goodbye, Ming," I said, crying, unable to control my tears.

"Go well, Od. May the road be kind to you, son."

With that, he opened the gate for me as I went outside the house. I could see Phichit waiting for us inside a Toyota Tacoma. We entered into his pickup truck and drove away.

I turned to look at Bat Erdene's house one last time, remembering Ming's words, "May the road be kind to you, son."

I closed my eyes and said "Amen" in the voice of Arban, Khulan, Qara, and in the name of all I have lost and loved, hoping that with their blessings, the seasons we were running into would find us with freedom.

Daddy's Curse 3

Get Your Hands on This E-Book & Find Out Today!

"Word-of-mouth is crucial for any author to succeed. If you enjoyed the book, please leave a review on my <u>Amazon review page</u>, even if it is just a sentence or two. It would make all the difference"